ASHIK KUMAR SATHEESH

Make Your Film

*How we made a Feature Film for $7,000 on an
iPhone SE and became a Film Director*

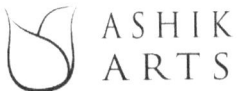

ASHIK
ARTS

First published by Ashik Arts LLP 2021

First edition

This book was professionally typeset on Reedsy.
Find out more at reedsy.com

*Dedicated with love and gratitude to
you, my dear fellow filmmaker!*

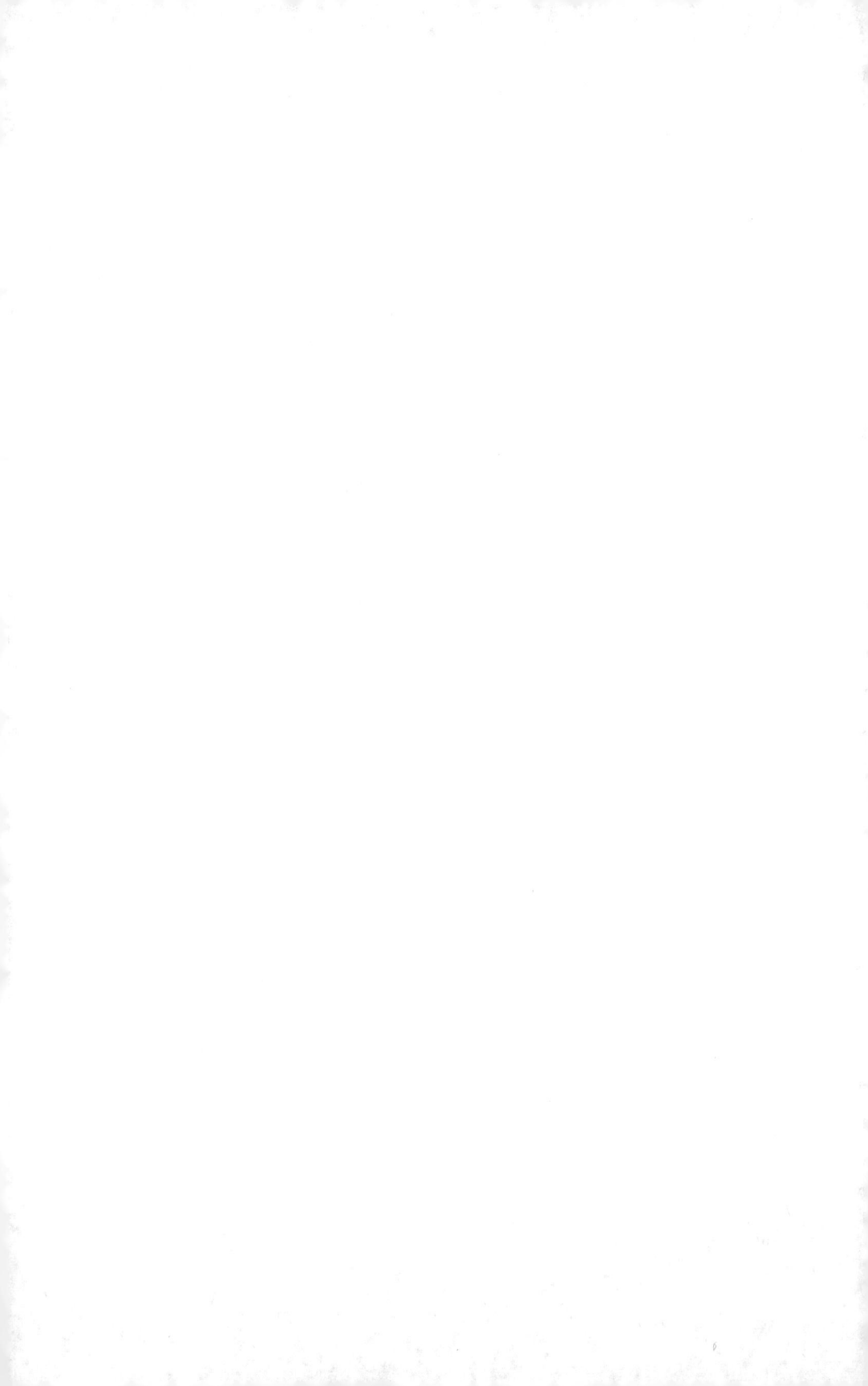

Contents

Preface

Filmmakers are living in a time of change. A time like none other, because no time in history has film production ever been this accessible to everyone. Being in such unchartered times can be challenging for some, and an opportunity for those ready to take it.

All good resources available on filmmaking were around Hollywood. Any credible information on how to make your feature film in India was almost impossible to find. Information for regional industry was non-existent.

This book is **best suited for** people who are looking to do the following:

- **Make a film for a low budget** and not wait for the date of a big star, or large sums of money from a producer
- Learn the dos and don'ts of **smartphone filmmaking**
- Send their film to festivals or release it on OTT platforms like Amazon **Prime**

Over the last many years I learnt filmmaking by experience, from books, videos, workshops and so on. Wading my way through in such changing times, we made our debut feature film, the first milestone for all filmmakers.

By sharing my experience through this book, I hope to give you, my fellow aspiring filmmaker, a framework of making your own film independently in India, whichever region you may be from. I hope it also gives you ideas I have learnt on selling and marketing it and make a living. I hope this book shines a light on the boulders that can drown you and also guides you though safe passes that I have discovered.

Ashik Kumar Satheesh
  Kerala, India
  July 2020

Acknowledgement

This book would not have existed had I not left my job and went in pursuit of making a living doing what I am most passionate about. I am thankful to all the challenges I faced, the objections and rejections I heard. Through those I realised how much I desired for the life I lead now.

I am grateful to all the great people who lit my way through their books, videos and life. It is because of such visionaries, that I could keep walking, in the hope of finding this light at the end of the darkness.

This book is what it is because of the efforts of two of my friends, Manu Adams and Harshitha S, who sat with me through days and months of reviewing. On top of that, it is the feedback of my filmmaking friends who read and critiqued the earlier drafts of this book that elevated it beyond what I could have ever done alone.

Eternally grateful to all my family, friends, and friends of friends, who supported us and made our debut film and this book possible.

1

Introduction

Before we get into the meat of the book, let me take a moment to introduce myself to you. I believe this would give you a better understanding of why I made some of the choices I made.

Who am I?

A curious and confused boy, who wanted to be a photographer, but became an engineer and finally ended up becoming a filmmaker.

I remember the first time I got a stills camera in my hand. It was my uncle's wedding. I was so eager. A little kid of 5 or 7, going around the *mandapam* lavishly taking 24 great photos on the film roll. When the photos came from the lab later, my mother mocked me. None of the photos had my uncle's or aunt's heads. I could only reach till their waists. Ah! Lesson one.

Deciding to Buy an SLR

I did not know then, but I would have to wait 13 years before I got my first SLR camera. It was on the eve of Christmas of 2010 that my parents and I bought my first ever SLR, a Nikon D3100 with an interchangeable 18 mm to 55 mm kit lens. A whole new world of photography opened up for me instantly.

When Photography Becomes a Limitation

At some point I felt limited by my ability to capture stories in one frame. The Nikon D3100 had a tiny little feature that let me record HD videos. I did fiddle around with it at times, more for fun than anything.

Even as a kid I loved getting in my hands on my father's friend's JVC and Sony HandyCam. I loved seeing the world reflected on its screen. More than anything, I loved the 'zoom'!

I always had a thing for writing, even from school days. It was far and few and too close to my heart to be shared with anyone but the closest of my closest friends. It was the naked truth of my life and I was not comfortable sharing with strangers. I would spend hours writing but only feel like I had spent minutes (the same happened whenever I was retouching photos). Over the years, with positive feedback from my friends, I started sharing my writings outside my comfort zone.

So while in college I wrote a script, got together with 3 of my friends and we made a short film. No, it did not take the world by storm. I shared it with my friends on Facebook. One of the comments said it had potential and that I should explore more. I don't even remember who said it, but I loved it and it ignited a tiny spark in my mind to try.

Adolescence to Adulthood

During this time I had finished college and life's challenges were taking over. I wanted to explore photography, I wanted to travel and see the world, to write, to study, to make music (I used to play the keyboard). I did not know what I wanted to do with my life.

I joined Tata Consultancy Services (TCS) as a Software Engineer in Mumbai. I kept exploring photography on the weekends. But something in me had changed and photography was not as exciting as it used to be.

Finding a Home

Never in my farthest dreams did I think that what I learned in attempting to improve my photography would come to use in a corporate environment. Within TCS itself, I found a group that satisfied my learning and exploration urges. We primarily handled documentation, training, video tutorials and so on. Here I got to fine-tune a lot of my skills—writing, teaching, public speaking and design. I felt like I found a home.

When The Home Became a Limitation

My desire to explore the depths of what I could do, grew bigger than what was possible there. It was all muddied, confusing and scary. But what gave courage was the surprising application of something I learned following my passion in a totally unrelated situation. This was invaluable in helping me believe that I could find use for anything I was about to take on. And I believed it.

The Vagabond

And so in 2015, at the age of 25, with a First Class degree in Electronics and Communication Engineering, and three years of work experience in a Multi National Company like TCS, I walked away from all of it. I decided to pursue art.

After leaving my job, I went hitchhiking across India. For six months I travelled to all the four corners of India. I was "soul searching" to say, or perhaps "lost" might be a better term. I still did not know what to do in life.

To relieve some of the pressures I wrote travelogues. This had a viewership beyond anything I have ever had till that point in my life. I got a call from one of my grandmothers, an English teacher. She had read it and said that my writing had potential. Interestingly, till that point, I had not thought of writing as a career path. But when an English teacher herself said that, something struck me.

I was sitting on the floor of an ashram in Guwahati. I was staying there for free as I travelled. Sitting there, I decided writing is my path. I decided to pursue a career as an author, to turn my novels into screenplays, and slowly build contacts in the film industry. And then make my own film some ten years down the line.

Becoming a Filmmaker

> "I always try to stress to people that there's a lot of work involved and years of preparation. But no one wants to hear that part."—Richard Linklater

I returned to my parents' house in Kochi, Kerala. I told them my plan and asked them to support me for two or three years, while I wrote my books. I made another short film with my family and few friends

4

who were still in Kochi. I assisted others' short films. I drafted another screenplay and made another short film, this time with a crew. I also assisted a feature film, which would go on to win countless awards and even bag that year's state award for the best feature film from Kerala. All the while I was developing the ideas of what was to became the book you are reading.

By 2018 I had a firm grasp on storytelling and had written some hundred partially formed story ideas. I had developed ten of these into complete stories, or treatments. From these ten treatments, I wrote fully fleshed-out screenplays for three. One of them I knew we could rewrite and make for $7,000 (₹ 5,00,000) and that became *Munnariv*, my debut feature film.

Jack of All Trades

My life might not be the most straightforward story out there. I thought my passion was to become a photographer, then an engineer, an author, a cinematographer, a musician, a traveller, an entrepreneur, a teacher, a leader, a film editor, a blogger, and whatnot. I was utterly clueless.

I envy those people who realise very early on what they want to do their whole life. My mother always knew she wanted to be a doctor, even when she was in preprimary! I knew nothing of what I wanted to do till I was 25! And you can imagine, this wasn't very pleasing for my mother. But what I did not realise then, but am eternally grateful that I can see this now, is that my diverse and varied interests is my biggest asset.

If you think of it, what exactly does a film director do? He or she doesn't write stories, or act, or set up the camera and the lights, or capture the sounds, or edit the film, or compose music, or do makeup, or design costumes and sets. They do nothing on set, but hold a vision for what they want and direct everyone towards it.

I want you to know that you do not have to have everything figured out right now. I spent the first 25 years of my life not knowing what I wanted to do, or become. I did not know what I was put on earth to do, or what impact I wanted to have on this world. I felt like a boat that went whichever way the wind blew or whatever I found interesting at that point.

Following the things that interested me, and having the courage to leave good things behind have always lead me onto something better. My life feels exuberant today because of the shadowy days I walked through, and the wonderful friends and family members that held me and guided me.

Making Space for the Future

I gave away the safety of my job to explore my skills as an artist. I gave up photography, cinematography and editing to be able to work with people who are far more passionate and talented than me. I give away everything I learned through this book, so that I can learn more advanced filmmaking techniques. And if it helps more people get to make their first feature film, nothing like it.

Forever an exploration!

* * *

Shyam Wants to be a Film Director, But

A friend of mine wanted me to talk to a friend of his. Let's call this guy Shyam. Shyam wants to be a film director. He works in Kochi while partnering with a writer to develop a script for his debut feature film.

Wow! Inspiring, is it not? Very similar to my story and aspirations as well. Or I thought. Interestingly my friend wanted me to talk Shyam out of wanting to be a film director! I was surprised by the request, for I am not a fan of talking anyone out of anything. Nonetheless I went to meet Shyam. And then I understood why my friend wanted me to dissuade him from filmmaking.

Shyam and Me

Shyam had very relatable aspirations like I had. But had an entirely different world view. Even how we carried ourselves were at opposite ends.

Shyam was a regular looking guy, probably in his late thirties. He had a receding and greying hairline. His hair was unkempt and stubble was overgrown. The first few buttons of his checkered shirt were undone. The shirt was untucked and loosely hung above his light blue faded jeans. His black sandals showed wear and tear.

On the other hand I was dressed in the best of my clothes. A well ironed solid shirt in teal. Sleeves neatly rolled up to the elbow. Tucked into an indigo blue jeans. A pair of slightly worn out gym shoes. Though my memory fails me, I would probably have had a shaven face, with a handlebar moustache.

The surprise in his eyes when he first saw me was evident. I was not what he was expecting. Maybe he read the same on my face as well, though I doubt it. We sat down on the steps of Marine Drive, looking out into the evening sky. The trees shaded us from the heat and the light sea breeze kept us refreshed. We got talking.

Shyam Wants to be a Film Director

Great! But he has never made a short film. Oh, okay. That was strange in this day and age. Though he hadn't made short films, he did have experience as a theatre director. Now, that's a start. Maybe he was at an earlier stage in his filmmaking career. Maybe he was a writer like me. So I enquired more.

Shyam wants to be a film director, but has never written a script. Oh yes! He did say that he had a writer writing the script for him. Writing a script requires a certain set of skills. Asking someone skilled in that to develop one's story was very common. So he had come up with the story I thought. It turns out he hadn't.

Shyam wants to be a film director and so he had a writer writing the script, not on a story he had developed, but on a One Line he had developed. A One Line is a commonly used tool in script development.

For example, take this One Line, "A computer hacker learns from mysterious rebels about the true nature of his reality and his role in the war against its controllers." Nothing that makes you go "ah-ha", is there? Coming up with that and coming up with the script of The Matrix is not the same thing.

Shyam Will Hire Talented People

Shyam wants to be a film director, but did not know anything about cameras or cinematography. To prove his point, he even narrated a story. A friend had sent him to a film set. There the cameraman asked Shyam to fetch the '50'. As it was the cameraman that was asking him Shyam had the intelligence to figure out that it was probably about a lens. But Shyam did not know what it looked like, or how to identify one.

A good point that Shyam told me was he need not know anything about cameras or lenses or cinematography, because he has a well experienced cinematographer friend who was going to be the cameraman for his debut film. Maybe he was an actor's director like Prakash Raj or Clint Eastwood and not a technical one. Fair enough.

One major difference in directing a film over a stage play is the immense power a director has in controlling the audience's perception, and thereby their emotions, merely by changing where the camera is placed and how the footage is edited together. I showed him a video I had made on how an editor tells a story. You cannot tell stories through films, unless you know the basics of film editing.

Shyam said he need not know all this, because he is going to hire experienced associate directors and editors and pay them well. They will know how to shoot a scene and edit it together. Shyam wants to be a film director, but did not know how to shoot a scene, or edit it together. By this point my dear friend Shyam was starting to get on my nerves.

If he had a talented writer who can develop a great story from just a line, experienced actors who can act, a cinematographer who captures the actor's performance, associate directors telling all of them what to do, and an editor to put together the film, I asked then what he was going to be doing on set. To which he said he will be the 'director'.

Where Shyam and I Are The Same

Why I have written Shyam's case in such detail is because everything he says is what I say too. In fact most of what he said is what you hear from all aspiring filmmakers. I too will work on my screenplay and develop it to its highest potential. We will work with more experienced technicians and fill gaps in our knowledge. All of us will go from one producer to another till we find that one producer who believes in us and the script. We will all learn on the job and become better filmmakers. One can only chase those dreams that one believes in. We all need to be rational optimists.

Being an Irrationally Optimist

Shyam was the most irrationally optimist wannabe film director I have ever met.

> *"Essentially, to create things, you have to be a rational optimist. Rational in the sense that you have to see the world for what it really is. And yet you have to be optimistic about your own capabilities, and your capability to get things done."—Naval*

Shyam wants to be a film director. I asked him why any producer should fund his project. Shyam said because the script was brilliant. I asked him if the script was indeed that brilliant, why wouldn't the producer buy the script and get an experienced director. Shyam said because it was his story. Yeah, 20 words from a 17,000 word script.

I asked him why anyone should bet their money on him, someone who has never made a film or even a short film, who doesn't know how to cover a scene or which lens to use, or anything about story or story structure or storytelling. To which he says because he will stand by the producer, be with the project till the very end and deliver a product. Probably.

I wanted him to think from a producer's point of view. So I asked Shyam if he wanted to build a house, how would he choose a contractor? Say a contractor approached Shyam and told him that he can build the house, but has never built a house, or even a shed. Would Shyam give all his hard earned money to that contractor? Trust him to build a house that he can someday leave to his children?

Where Shyam and I Are Different

I don't think he quite got what I meant. He kept saying something like he will learn film direction on the job from all the experienced people he would hire for his debut film. With that experience he would then go on to make a better second film, then a third and so on and he would become a film director. He strongly believes that he can find someone to trust him and put in $1,000,000 (or ₹ 1,00,00,000) so that he can learn filmmaking. What he was actually telling me was that he does not want to do the work of learning filmmaking unless someone payed him.

My world view is that I work first and then I get payed. My past several years have been dedicated entirely to developing my skills as a storyteller, working days and nights, studying, implementing, learning from mistakes, and making short films. Heck, I even made a feature film on a mobile phone to build my knowledge and credibility! Even then I am always concerned if I have learned enough. I know that I know few things, but lots left to learn. I am also aware that there are infinitely more things that I don't even know I don't know.

My friend Manu used to tell me that I am a 'practical dreamer'. I don't think I quite grasped the entirety of what he meant until I met an impractical dreamer. That said,

> "It's probably better to be an irrational optimist, than it is to be a rational cynic."—Nivi

Shyam Can Become a Film Director

Rational cynics are those who "will not only never do anything great in their lives, they'll prevent other people around them from doing something great. They think their job is to shoot holes in things... They want to tell you why the thing is not going to work."

No, Shyam wasn't a rational cynic. He was an optimist with high hopes and dreams. It's just that to me it seemed irrational and unrealistic. You never know.

> "It's unrealistic to bend a piece of metal and fly people over the ocean in that metal. Luckily the Wright Brothers and Benjamin Franklin didn't think so."—Will Smith

Shyam might in fact find that one person with money who will fund his debut film. Maybe his script is really that great, and he will quickly grasp film direction from that one film and make his second and third films. Shyam can become a film director. There is that 1% probability that it can happen, that luck can strike. I believe in putting in the work and making my luck.

> "In 1,000 parallel universes, you want to be wealthy [or a film director, or fill in whatever you want to be] in 999 of them. You don't want to be wealthy in the 50 of them where you got lucky. We want to factor luck out of it."—Naval

Listening to Shyam's beautiful dreams I did not want to be the rational cynic. He asked if I can be an associate director on his film. I politely asked him to call me if his work starts. I wished Shyam all the best and left.

Shyam wants to be a film director, but doesn't want to do the hard work. Don't be a Shyam. In fact you taking the time to read this book and learn proves to me you are not a Shyam. Now let's get started.

* * *

How To Break Into The Film Industry

The way you are going to break into the film industry is by answering this question, "What are you really good at that the film industry values, according to you and others?"

Is it in creating beautiful frames and capturing defined shadows? Is it in designing a soothing soundscape that the audience can melt into? Is it in creating wonderful characters and stories around them that people can see themselves in? Is it in becoming a character and portraying it masterfully in front of a camera?

What Are You Good At?

You have to choose. And choose not only based on your own observations, but also based on what others whom you trust tell you you are good at. Then you know you are not bluffing yourself.

If you think of my own story, I decided to become a writer not only because I had an interest in it. But I found people who are experts in the field who corroborated what I felt. I pursued filmmaking when others seeing what I had created felt I had potential.

If you are good at it, you will keep doing it, over and over. Making your own mistakes. To be able to make your own mistakes you need to be in those positions where you can experiment. A writer needs to be writing scripts/stories, an actor needs to be on set/stage acting, a film director needs to be telling stories through film and so on. Then you will find what works for you and what doesn't. You'll find what the industry wants and doesn't. Let us take the case of an actor as it is easier to grasp and people get it.

How to Break Into The Film Industry as an Actor

If you are an aspiring actor only waiting for an opportunity to act, then you are probably doing it wrong. If you are not getting cast in feature films, then find theatre groups nearby and act in that. Acting is acting, be it in films, theatre, ads or wherever.

"The separation of talent and skill is one of the greatest misunder-stood concepts for people who are trying to excel, who have dreams, who want to do things. Talent you have naturally. Skill is only developed by hours and hours and hours of beating on your craft." - Will Smith

If even theatres are not hiring find people who are making short films and act in that. If no one is casting you in short films, even after offering to act for free, or driving them around, or offering to buy their food, then you need to really ask yourselves the question "why".

Have you done the work? Have you studied acting? Have you stood in front of an audience/camera and believably became a character? What can you show to make the director trust you to deliver a satisfactory result on screen?

Breaking in Faster

If you need things to happen faster, write your own short stories and create your own short films. Convince your jobless friend who is interested in photography with the latest camera to shoot your short film over the weekend. If no friend will help out, do it solo.

In 1995 nobody was casting Vin Diesel (of *Fast & Furious*). He needed to do something and out of his frustration he directed a short film about bring a frustrated actor. It was seen by Steven Spielberg and cast him in *Saving Private Ryan* and you know where he is now.

If it is a filmmaker you want to be, you can either be creatively coming with excuses—the producer isn't giving money, or the actor didn't give you dates, or someone stole the script—or you can make a film. In this day and age, if you are not making films on your own, you are only fooling yourself. If we can do it, so can you. If you absolutely **need** something, you will in time find a way. Else it is only something you would **like** to have.

> *"Filmmakers are going to make films, just like painters are going to paint."—Richard Linklater*

We need to learn to take responsibility and accountability of where we need to be and work towards it. If you do not do that, nothing bad is going to happen to you. Trust me. You will safely remain where you are, dreaming of a so and so life, forever.

Take The Risk on Yourself

Be in those places where you have to make it happen or die. If you can't put your whole life on line for what you believe you are good at, and what other trustworthy people tell you are good at, you are not ready.

Few years back an aspiring actor was dead broke. He wasn't getting cast in any role anywhere. He attempted to write screenplays, so that he could then act in it. For one of those scripts he wrote, a studio offered him $125,000, but they did not want to cast him in the role. He turned it down.

The studio wanted the script and offered him $250,000. His wife had left him. He had to sell his dog, his only companion, for $300 to even keep himself fed. He was that broke and still he said no, because he knew where he needed to be and was ready to get there or die trying.

The studio raised their offer to $325,000 and still he turned it down. So the studio finally agreed. They paid him only $35,000 and cast him. The film went on to win that year's Oscars, including being nominated for best actor and screenplay. His career skyrocketed from there, spanning borders and become one of the biggest action heroes. You guessed it right. The film's name was *Rocky* and the actor was none other than Sylvester Stallone.

You Will Break Into The Film Industry

Build up your knowledge and break your fears one by one. Expand your comfort zone, little by little. Eventually people will give you whatever resources you need. Directors will cast you because you have now built a following and trust that you can deliver on screen. Producers will give you the money to go make your film because you've earned the money back in your previous films. A star will give you dates because people seem to always fall in love with your characters in every one of your films.

And because of all the works you've done, the mistakes you've made, the lessons learnt, the skills you acquired, when that opportunity comes, you will have honed your craft so well that you can take it on without fear and deliver.

Pick something that the industry values that you are really good at, not only according to you but also according to others whom you trust. Keep doing it with conviction and courage, building up your skill and confidence. If you are doing something that you love that the industry wants, it is inevitable that you find your place and break in.

* * *

Becoming a Feature Film Director

Almost all aspiring filmmakers hope to some day make their debut into the world of feature films. They might be working in Ads, music videos, short films, corporate work and so on, but for almost a century, success as a feature film director has been seen as the height of a career in the film industry.

With modern sensitive digital cameras and easy access to postproduction softwares, filmmaking is no longer the staple of a few. Earlier it was not possible to enter into the filmmaking world but by assisting someone, building contacts, getting a producer or a star to say yes and so on. But now the barrier of entry is almost zero. In the olden days it was impossible for anyone to make a film for nothing because there was always going to be the costs of the film roll, its development and so on.

"Technology has levelled the playing field; a boon and a bane."

Nowadays every other person with a camera is a creator. The world has never seen so much of content being produced, ever. Not only in the form of films, but also as photos on Instagram, 15 second videos on TikTok, games, web series, micro blogs on Twitter and so on. All of which are vying for the same thing, your attention. Even this book.

Though this is the reality of the situation, anything that adds value in the form of what one is seeking, will always find a place. A good story will always find its listener, a good book will find its readers. The audience for it might be millions, or maybe just one.

The films you create now are in stiff competition, with films in its industry, from the nearby industry, and from all film industries of the world. It is also in competition with the 9 year old boy's SnapChat feed and at the same time with the most widely played game in the world.

"During a content overflow time like now, it is imperative that the films you create are of the best craft possible."

And the only possible way to hone your craft, in any field, is by doing it over and over. But how do you hone your craft making feature films, when you can't even make one?

Independent Filmmaking

One way of making your debut into the filmmaking world is to find someone who believes in you to put in huge sums of their wealth. For most people who are starting out this is not going to happen. It is startling to see the number of people who believe that they can do this, Shyams, because they read about someone somewhere who did this.

If I believed I could walk into a producer's office with no credibility and walk out with a film gig I would not be writing this. If you believed in it you would not be reading this either. So now that we have crossed that out of our list, let me tell you how you can hone your craft to become a feature film director, without huge sums of money from a producer, or the dates of a big star, or VFX and such gimmicks.

To me the answer was to make an low budget film.

* * *

What is a Low Budget Film?

Indie, independent, low budget, no budget, micro budget, ultra low budget, available resource filmmaking—these are all confusing terms that mean various things to various people in various parts of the world. For example, a Low Budget Film of Hollywood, is a Big Budget Film in my state (Kerala, India) and a Mega Budget Film for someone in Africa.

So let us define low budget filmmaking as the process of making a film where your budget allows only for spending on the essentials. The budgets for a low budget film can be anything from nothing, to just paying for food and travel, to differed payments to the crew, to half rates for everyone and so on. But nobody is being given hefty payments and your crew is not going to be in hundreds, but maybe 10 or 20.

Pros of Making a Low Budget Film

If you do decide to make a low budget film, then you stand to gain the following:

- **Self reliance**
  Once you've made a film for almost nothing, compared to a normal film's budget, you gain confidence in yourself. You now know for certain that no matter what, you can inspire a handful of other artists and pull together an entire feature film, with or without the support of an industry. You cannot gain that any other way.
- **Creative freedom**
  Neither is there a producer you need to please, nor an audience. The only person you need to please is yourself. The freedom this allows you to experiment is unparalleled.
- **Quick turn around**
  As you do not have a huge crew, you can steer your production to try out new horizons that you could not have anticipated earlier.

Let me not just paint a rosy picture.

Cons of Making Low Budget Film

The following are the thorns that can hurt you:

- **Extremely demanding**
  Making a low budget film is going to test you like no other film you

may make. It is going to demand every ounce of your strength, will power and persistence to pull through it. Especially so if it is your debut feature. You do not have the ally of money to solve problems. There will be moments where you would want to throw your hands up and leave. It is only your creativity, drive and the team that can take your through those.

- **Strenuous on connections**
  It can be extremely demanding of your connections, both profes-sional and personal. Your team is not going to be paid much, but they too have families to look after. They could be doing something elsewhere and making more money. But they choose to be there. It is also demanding on you personal connections as every day of the shoot, my parents' house was full of people. It was my parents who made breakfast for them everyday. The house was a mess, throughout the shoot and even into postproduction.

Test the waters of low budget filmmaking with lesser demanding short films before diving into a feature film.

Implications on The Film

Now that you know what the pros and cons of making a low budget film are, here are other things to consider:

- **No theatre distribution** It is less likely that a traditional distributor is going to want the film. They need stars to sell tickets. Unless you are yourself a star, or you somehow got a big name actor to act in your film, your film is going to be released through online platforms and festivals.
- **No publicity** No news channel is going to follow you or your film around. You will have to build awareness and desire for your film by

marketing it yourself. If you are in for the fame, you are better off making a regular budget star studded film.

- **No grand locations** Your film is not going to have exotic locations, or dance pieces. In fact it is probably only going to have a handful of locations, either those that you own, or that your friends and family does, or free public ones.
- **No special effects, VFX** Your film is not going to have any spectacular tricks. No space rockets, no hi-fi gadgets or stunts or set pieces.
- **Smaller version of the film** You might have written a script a certain way, but if you want to make it yourself, you might have to rewrite making compromises. Your film might not be as grand as you dreamt it to be.
- **Not everyone is going to love it** And because of all of the above, your film might not look and sound like a traditional film that normal audiences are used to. Hence not everyone is going to love it.

Take these only as guidelines. If your story needs VFX and you can do spellbinding visual effects then of course your film will have those. But because you do not have the money to hire others, you would have to do it all on your own, or spend more time instead. What I mean to say is that you cannot have all of these without budgets for that. If you want one, you will have to sacrifice something else. If your story needs a lot of locations then you might have to pay more for travel, need more shoot days, more money for food and so on.

Indie Films That Did It Right

If you think these restrictions are going to make nothing but boring film, you need to watch Robert Rodriguez[1]'s debut independent film *El Mariachi*. It was made by just a one-man-crew, the director himself, when he was 23 years old. Even Christopher Nolan's first film was a low budget indie, called *Following*.

Now that you know the pros and cons of making a spectacular low budget film in spite of the what the implication of the budget can be, let's prepare to make one.

* * *

---

[1] If you looking to make a debut feature as a low budget film, I highly recommend reading Robert Rodriguez's book Rebel Without a Crew.

2

What It Takes

Most aspiring filmmakers start by making short films. Short film are to me a place to horn one's skills in preparation for a feature. When I was making them I used to wonder how different making a feature film would be.

Feature Film vs Short Film

The question of whether I should make a feature film or a short film next is one that all aspiring filmmakers face. Let me share with you some of the differences between making a feature and a short film.

Duration

This one is obvious of course. A short film is short and a feature film is long. But what is not so obvious is what exactly short and long means. There is no universal standard as of now. In the US, Academy of Motion Picture Arts and Sciences defines feature length as over 40 minutes while India's Central Board of Film Certification (CBFC) defines any film of more than 72 minutes as long. Most film festival submissions require a minimum duration of 40 or 60 minutes for feature films. For short films, the minimum duration can be even in seconds.

There is no standard whatsoever for the maximum duration for feature films. As Indians we are used to seeing 3 hour long films. Even today most Indians consider 90 minutes film to be a short film. But anywhere outside of India, 90 minutes is the average length you would find features in.

If you are looking for festivals, it is better to keep your film around 90 minutes. It is easier for them to program a 1.5 hour long film than a 2 or 3 hour one. Which is not to say such films cannot make it in festivals. But generally that is what is suggested, unless you are an already established film director.

Sweet spot? 80 to 100 minutes.

Budget

A feature film is going to need a lot more resources than a short film. By resources I do not just mean money, but also time and crew. A short requires less of everything. It also does not need big marketing budgets either. Not only does a feature film take more time in production, but also in all the stages of writing, pre-production, post-production, marketing and so on.

Release

Probably a short film is not going to be released theatrically. It might play at a few festivals and then end up on YouTube or some online platform. You might also be able to sell it on Video-On-Demand (VOD) platforms, or as DVDs. But not many are likely to purchase as they can get a lot more value for money from features, at least as of now. The advantage of releasing a short on a platform like YouTube is that it might go viral and gain you viewership that make theatricals look petite.

Return

Features can collect money by releasing online, winning at festival, running in theatres, airlines, TV, radio, DVD, Blu-Ray, selling music, making remakes, dubbed versions, and various other ways. We pay and consume feature films through such ways. Whereas paying for short film is almost unheard of.

Recognition

It is not likely that any actor is going be a star by acting in a short film. It might get them an opportunity to act in feature films. Historically, stars, fame and recognition have been part of feature films on the big screen. Though interestingly this was not the case right after films were born. During those days 'film' only meant short films, and people who acted in them were popular.

Stories

The big one for me is that the longer the duration of a film, the more nuanced I can make the characters. It is difficult to show the different sides of more than one character in a short film. Even showing conflicting aspects of one character in a short film requires mastery of the craft.

Whereas features have the time to explore such deeper conflicts. TV and Web Series offer an even wider canvas, granted you can craft an engaging story. Think of it like short stories, novellas and novels. All have different scopes and purposes and people expect different things from each of them. That said, shorts let a director explore more freely.

And hence shorts need not always deliver a cohesive story as compared to a feature film that is meant to be consumed in theatres.

So Should I Make a Feature Film or a Short Film?

Only you can answer that. You will know once you are ready. Most of the points above would be obvious. But weigh yourself on each of these. A feature is going to demand a lot more on each of these than a short. Let us look at what all you need to make your debut feature film.

* * *

7 Steps to Make Your First Feature Film

The easiest, fastest and safest way to reach a goal is to follow someone who is already there. When I was starting out as a filmmaker, I searched everywhere to know the steps I needed to take. All the established filmmakers were far ahead from where I was—an absolute newbie starting out with nothing but passion. Their baby steps were unrepeatable.

So here for you are the 7 steps I followed to make my first feature film, without a star or big budgets:

1. I decided to be a filmmaker
2. Learned and made short films
3. Connected with like minded people
4. Worked on sets
5. Wrote and rewrote scripts
6. Raised funds
7. Made our film happen

Just so you know, this took me four and a half years. Have patience. It might work faster for you or slower. You might not need some of these steps, or you might need different ones altogether. But having a framework that worked can help you find your own way. Let us look at these in some more detail.

* * *

Deciding to be a Filmmaker

Deciding to be a filmmaker might have been, for me, the hardest step of all. This is my personal journey. Your journey might not be anything like mine. But I hope this lets you know that you are not alone.

Adding onto what you read in the previous chapter, I come from a family of working class men and women—teachers, doctors, advocates—for whom arts was something to pass time with. And not something to make a living out of.

I walked out of college with job offers in two Multinational Companies, while my colleagues with Distinguished Engineering certificates were unable to secure even one. For someone who had never earned in his life, the pay was good. New city, new friends, New experiences. And within TCS itself getting to work on things that interested me, it was all fun. Life was good.

Deciding to Quit

When everything is good, why quit? That is exactly why deciding to be a filmmaker was the hardest for me. Unlike the cliche story of someone hating their job and deciding to follow their passion, I loved what I did. And I was good at it too.

I was happy and so was everyone else. Deciding to leave that, to jump into the unknown, was tough. What prompted me to make the jump was something in me that kept saying that I could be more. I wasn't using the full potential of who I was. Nor was a position higher in the corporate ladder going to do that.

> *"It is in your moments of decision that your destiny is shaped."* — Tony Robbins

It might seem unbelievable now, but I did not know then that it is a filmmaker that I wanted to be. I knew I wanted to do something in the arts, probably writing. And through that maybe in 5/10 years, find my way to becoming a film director. All I knew was that I loved stories. And I jumped in.

"You can't connect the dots looking forward; you can only connect them looking backwards. So you have to trust that the dots will somehow connect in your future." Steve Jobs

Your Journey to be a Filmmaker

The conviction of knowing to the very core of our being why I am here, who I am meant to be, that is the only thing that will keep you going when things are not going the way you wanted them to. Spend time to find your reasons. It is worth putting down our life for.

It was only that which gave me the courage to convince my near and dear ones, held me strong when my distant family members criticised, kept me aligned to my goals when the paths faltered. I pray that you find your calling and the courage to follow through to a joyful and purpose driven life.

* * *

Learning Filmmaking

Learning filmmaking is very easy. Its basics are so simple that Robert Rodriguez (the director of films like Spy Kids, Sin City, Desperado) can teach it to you in 10 minutes!

I do not know if you realise that pre-internet, if you wanted to study something, the only options were to apprentice with a master, or apply with a school, or go digging through heaps of books in a library. But now we can just snap away and learn anything, when and where we want to.

The Important Aspect of Learning Filmmaking

> *"You are not going to learn from just watching movies. You'll learn somethings. You'll learn more, picking up the camera, by making your own films, your own mistakes."* — *Robert Rodriguez*

I have read everything I could find online about filmmaking. I've seen almost every tutorial I could on filmmaking (exaggerating of course). But that is nothing compared to what I learned by making my first 2 minute short film with my friends.

No one has ever learned to swim without drowning a little. You do not learn swimming reading books or watching the latest tech review on swimwear. If you take away anything from this, I hope it is that you write a story, pick up your phone, shoot it, edit it, show it to people and listen. Their reactions will tell you how good or bad your filmmaking is.

Your Short Films Suck

I guarantee that. One of my earliest attempts to make a comedy short film was an utter failure. Your work will fail too. To that, I say to you what the radio show host Ira Glass spoke on the creative process,

*"Everybody I know who does interesting creative work went through a phase of years, where they could tell what they were making wasn't as good as they wanted it to be... It's totally normal and the most important possible thing you could do is [to] **do a lot of work,** because it's only by actually going through a volume of work that you're going to catch up and close that gap and the work you're making will be as good as your ambitions."* — Ira Glass

Learn, Do, Teach

This is my philosophy, in everything I do. Learn everything I can. Put it into practice to the best of my knowledge and abilities. And finally, teach. Even this book is part of that teaching phase. It forces me to analyse my mistakes and achievements, and systematically share it. Learn filmmaking, make films, and share.

* * *

One Thing to Do to Reach Your Goals

As I started writing the third step in my series of 7 steps to make your first feature film, I realised that in my journey there was a small step in between; taking the first step. For most people starting out, this is usually where they get stuck. So here is Scene 2A – The One Thing.

People do not take that first step for various reasons. For some it is the fear of failure, and for some that of success. The one thing that you need to do to make your first feature film is to take that first step. But what is that first step?

Where Are you?

After leaving my job, after my 6 month hiatus, when I returned home on the eve of the new year of 2016, I had nothing, but an idea to become a writer. It could have either ended up being an artsy-fartsy thing or something I'd have been proud of my whole life.

Whatever it may be that I want to do, it starts first and foremost, with me; wherever I am, with whatever I have, in that moment. That is the only place where anyone can start.

I could complain that I knew no one, that my parents didn't have the right connections or weren't rich. I could complain that the timing wasn't right, or that the filmmaking scene in my state wasn't good. I could complain about everything that is not right around me, or I could shut up, find that one thing I could do right now that'd get me where I want to be, and do that.

The One Thing

Once I had decided to become a filmmaker, learned filmmaking, made shorts, I sat down to do the one thing that I knew I had to do next; write stories. After that I did the next one thing I knew I had to do; turn one of those stories into a screenplay.

When you are clear on what you want, when you accept where you are and commit to the journey to your goals, all you need to know is the one thing that you need to do right now. For as soon as you do that, you will know what to do next.

Once I had the script, I knew exactly what I needed next; money for food, an actor, a cameraman, a sound guy and so on. Basically connections. What is the one thing you need to do right now to get to your goals?

* * *

Connecting With Like Minded People

Connecting with like minded people is a must in filmmaking than any other art form. Painter and writers can go to a shop and buy the raw materials they need to make their art. But a filmmaker needs people, with a variety of skills.

"Everything you want in life is a relationship away." Idowu Koyenikan

A Film Crew

A film absolutely needs people who can do the following:

- Come up with interesting characters and narrate an engaging series of incidents that happens to those characters, usually called a writer
- Bring those characters into life, in flesh and blood, usually called actors
- Capture what those actors are performing, usually called a camera-man
- Capture the actor's voices, and the sounds around, usually called a sound technician[2]

With the advent of technology a lot of these roles have become easier to do. One person may in fact do it all. But those kind of films are limited in scope. And if you are reading this, it is probably not the kind of films

---

[2] Are you wondering why there was no Director in the list of people absolutely necessary to make a film? If there is a solid script, if the actors know what to do, if the cameraman knows where to best place the camera, and there is a sound technician who knows to do his job, does a film really need a director?

you want to do.

>*"Alone we can do so little; together we can do so much."* —Helen
>Keller

Your Connections

Your friends, cannot act; unless they are studying acting and are
into it. Your friend who takes pretty pictures on SnapChat is not a
Cinematographer. You might be able to bring some of them together
and pull together a short film. But that will be an amateur work. But if
that is all that you can do right now, then by all means please do that. I
did that too.

When you want to take your work to the next level, you are going
to need professionals in all of these departments. And when you are
starting out, you are not going to be able to hire them. You either need
to have friends who are professionals, or you need to become friends
with professionals.

Connecting With Professionals

Never go to a professional, shake their hands, and ask them to work in
your film, that too for free. Most probably they'd politely say no and
back away. Instead invest in people who are going to be professionals in
the future. Ask your friends if they have friends who are studying in film
schools. Ask your family members if they know someone who knows
someone who acts. Go to film workshops. Meet people.

Make friends with people who are like you, starting out and some
day will be professionals. So when that day comes when you are
going to make your first feature, you would have friends who are then
professionals to help you out. Yes it takes time. Patience.

"I always had that long-term vision. Even getting going with cinema, knowing it was such a long road to be able to make films, but I always had a long term. Whenever I was starting out, I had that patience."—Richard Linklater

Connecting a Network of People

What you are building, is a network. Give it time. Give it a year, give it ten. Check in with them in between. See if you can be of any help to them. Send them books, tutorials, contests, any information that might help them get ahead in their journey. Bring them value first, through your skills, and connections.

"Networking is not about just connecting people. It's about connecting people with people, people with ideas, and people with opportunities." Michele Jennae

Whatever your journey might be, if there is one thing that might make you feel less alone, it is to share the walk with like minded people.

"If you want to go fast, go alone. If you want to go far, go together."
— African Proverb

This is also one of the reasons why I took time out from going onto my second feature to write this book, conduct workshops, record videos and so on. I want you to make your films. I want us all to be storyteller. If my journey somehow helps you in that, nothing like it.

* * *

Being an Assistant Director On Set

Working as an Assistant Director (AD) on set is a safe way for anyone starting out, to learn the actual workings of putting together a film. And maybe to earn some money at the same time. If it is feature films that you wish to make, be on feature film sets. If it is Ads that you wish to make, then be on Ad sets. Work where you wish to work.

Getting to be an Assistant Director

Culturally we are in a shift. A lot more content is being made right now all across the globe than any other time in history. For people starting out in this field that is good news. The need for more personnel could be your foot into the industry. Take the opportunity while it lasts. As of writing this, there are more films being made than there is time for people to watch. In economics whenever there is more supply than demand, the market corrects itself by reducing the price of goods. Which deters people from the producing goods. Which is to say, the filmmaking rush will diminish, then rise, then diminish and again and again and again.

When People Don't Let You Assist

You should know that even during rising times like these, Directors have turned down my offers to assist them. Why? Because they already have more than enough Assistant Directors. There is more supply than demand. But I did get to be an Assistant Director of two feature films, besides countless short films and Ads. I got all of those opportunities through the connections I had made.

You need to invest in yourself first and show that you know the craft through your work. Only when this creates enough faith in others, will they recommend you to someone; after all, it is their reputation that is on the line.

> *"Confidence and hard work is the best medicine to kill the disease called failure. It will make you a successful person."* — *Abdul Kalam*

Being On Set

Being an AD on set is tough. There is a lot of standing and running around. You are working a minimum of 12 to 16 hours a day and maybe sleeping for 5 or 6. But by being an assistant on others' sets I got to see things differently. I saw how each of them worked and found practices that I would like to adopt and those that I should never adopt.

Even more importantly, I found professionals point out my strengths and weaknesses. They saw things that I had never known in myself and nobody else could see.

Learning About Myself as an Assistant Director

On one of the sets the Assistant Cinematographer told me that he could see that I was going to make a feature film very soon. A makeup man once told me that he noticed that whenever there was a problem on set, I solved it immediately.

The incident he was talking about was a minor case of arranging transport for a junior actor. I had always been like that and so I did not think much of it. But later I realised why it was a strength. If I do not solve problems as and when they occur, they pile up. The more problems you have to solve at a time, the more it drains. Putting out a cigarette butt is way easier than trying to put out the forest fire it eventually created. I never left anyone's question unanswered or any requirement unattended for later. I got it cleared then and there, which I believe is a requirement for any director; in fact for any good leader in any field. I did not know these were my strengths.

For my weaknesses, I realised that logistics or handling too many people is not my area of comfort. Though I did learn to manage. Unfortunately that is a skill an AD on set must have, or at least as far as my experience has been. I am good at planning. I can sit down for hours in preproduction, go through the script and break it down to its atoms, foresee things that can go wrong and plan for contingencies. But I am not the high energy AD a set demands.

Everything comes down to knowing about yourself and others around you, so that you can partner up with people whose strengths are your weaknesses. And by working as an AD, wherever it may be that you wish to work, you will not only earn some money, but also learn filmmaking, about yourself, and build connections, meet technicians and make new friends.

* * *

Writing and Rewriting Scripts

Of all our 7 steps writing and rewriting scripts is something that you absolutely need to be doing.

> *"If your goal is to become a film director, you must master screenwriting." — Akira Kurosawa*

Why Non-Writers Should Write

Not everyone is a writer. Your dream might be to become a producer, a cinematographer, an actor, or any one of the other creative fields, and with no interest whatsoever in writing. Why then should you be writing scripts?

Whatever your passion might be, we are all storytellers. We have been hearing and telling stories since the time we were born. Every single human on the plant knows when they hear a good story. But very few can articulate why a story is good, and even fewer who can craft a beautiful one. Should you go ahead with a script? How do you identify if it has the potential to be reworked? How do you creatively criticise?

You need to understand what a story is, how a story is structured, and why stories work. There is a science to it, and of course an art to it. You may or may not have the art, but you can, and should, learn the science.

> *"Storytelling is powerful; film particularly. We can know a lot of things intellectually, but humans really live on storytelling. Primarily with ourselves; we're all stories of our own narrative."—Richard Linklater*

Writing is Rewriting

I have found that the process of rewriting is unglamorous and so is one of the least discussed topics in the scriptwriting world. But it is a fact that most people starting out does not realise. A script is never written. But it is rewritten.

"Secure writers don't sell first drafts. They patiently rewrite until the script is as director-ready, as actor-ready as possible. Unfinished work invites tampering, while polished, mature work seals its integrity." Robert McKee

I remember someone calling the first draft of a script as "the puke draft". It is like a certain rock, which if polished well can become a diamond. The diamond is what we all aim for.

It might take 2 rewrites, it might take 10. In each rewrite we attempt to bring out a more cohesive story, more rooted and relatable characters, find the tone of the story, its pacing. Sometimes a character becomes unnecessary, while at other times a new character might be needed. You might have to reimagine the ending, or perhaps even thrash the whole script. You may never know. Rewriting is unglamorous. But it is what writing is.

Rewriting for low budget films

For people making their first film on their own, there is an additional rewriting required. I rewrote *Munnariv* to make it in my bedroom. Generally, if your budget is less, it is better to rewrite the following out of the script:

- **Period stories** Stories happening in a time period other than right now, need props and costumes to be time accurate. Just take a simple item as the phone that the character would have. If your story happens in 2000s, you would then have to scout, and pay for one of those old flip phones.
- **Night scenes** Have as less of them as possible. Night scenes need lots of lighting to look good and be within the camera's noise level. Additional lighting takes time to setup, and a bigger crew. Moreover it is draining on all the crew members and you probably will have to schedule a break soon afterwards.
- **Crowds** You protagonist walking by a crowded lane? No problem. The protagonist walking by a lane and everyone slapping him, or jumping on him, or any such specific action? Unless you make the

actor do something stupid that a mob attacks him and thrashes him for real, not possible! The more the number of people you have on set, the more it is going to cost for food.

- **Animals** Animals you see in films are trained. They are accompanied by their trainers who get them to act. Your neighbour's dog is not going to do as you ask him to and when you want him to. Lest you have all the time in the world to catch that one time he does the action, rewrite animals out of the script. Of course if it is just one scene where an animal does something, retain it.
- **Kids** Similar to animals, kids are hard to manage. They can have unexpected mood swings and take a lot of time.
- **Guns** I learned this the hard way. I made a short film where the whole film revolved around a guy who was going to shoot himself. What I didn't realise till it was too late, was the prop gun we had felt like a prop gun. No one watching the short believed for a second that that gun was capable of killing him. The film fell flat, dead. I could not even release it. People are so used to seeing real guns in films that unless you can get one, rewrite it out.
- **Stunts** Please don't write car chases or big stunts into your low budget film. You are not going to be able to pull it off in a way that looks realistic. It will look amateurish, reveal that you did not have money and drag the audience out of the film. The film will loose it's worth.
- **Special effects, VFX** Same as stunts. Everyone is used to seeing good quality effects nowadays. Unless you are yourself a good VFX artist, you are not going to be able to pull it off in any way that looks acceptable.

Please take these only as guidelines. I do not mean to say that your film cannot have any of these. If your story absolutely needs a crowd scene, then by all means have it. But plan for it in advance. Have it included in your budget, find friends and family members who can be that crowd. Have a team of assistant directors to help you manage the crowd. And so on. Know that when you choose to retain any of these, you are adding a certain cost and risk factor to your film.

Anyway the point is that you should be writing scripts even while you are learning filmmaking, building your network, and assisting feature films. I was writing scripts even before I decided to be a full time filmmaker. Being a writer, it came easier for me. I hope I made a strong case on everyone learning the basic of writing. It is your only sure-fire way of getting a foot in the industry.

* * *

CrowdFunding a Low Budget Film

Funding might not be the most attractive thing for the creator in you, but is undeniably essential to make your debut film. I made calls to over a 100 of my friends and family members to raise funds for *Munnariv*.

Why Not Approach A Producer?

The truth is that I did not have the courage to. I did not have the confidence to sit in front of them and tell them that I can pull off a feature film. Probably my fear of rejection too was stopping me.

Though the same basic principles hold, I believe the craft required to hold someone's attention for 10 minutes in a short film, is different from entertaining and enlightening them for the length of a whole feature. I had the faith in me that I could do it, but nothing to prove it. Which also made me doubt myself if I actually can, if I would give up half way through.

These were the many reasons why I needed to make my first feature film just one step out of my comfort zone. I did not want to jump out with both my legs and lose hold of my footing, like I did when I quit my job and went travelling. Jumping into a full blown set, with a hundred people waiting for my decisions, when I myself was having doubts about my skills, would have been too much. So for me a low budget film was the way to go. For which I first needed to figure out a budget.

Budgeting a Low Budget Film

The budgeting of a a low budget film is a different game compared to a normal film. It's very simple actually. After all, you don't have any money except for:

- Food
- Travel

Rest everything you **beg, borrow** or **steal**. This is where all the efforts you put into the previous steps come into play. Sharing for you a screenshot of how we had made the initial budget allocation, so that you have a framework to start from.

	Budget	% of total
4k Cam, Lens, Filters	₹40,000.00	4.20%
Grip, Lights, Gimbal, Tripod	₹50,000.00	5.25%
Location Sound, Foley, Mix	₹50,000.00	5.25%
Expendables	₹25,000.00	2.62%
Props & wardrobe	₹25,000.00	2.62%
Transportation	₹50,000.00	5.25%
Food	₹60,000.00	6.30%
DCP, Censor	₹50,000.00	5.25%
	₹350,000.00	36.75%
Publicity	₹50,000.00	5.25%
Misc - Production	₹25,000.00	2.62%
Misc - Post	₹65,000.00	6.82%
Legal	₹25,000.00	2.62%
	₹140,000.00	14.70%
Payments	₹437,500.00	45.93%
Total (w/o differed)	₹575,375.00	60.41%
Total (including Differed)	₹952,500.00	100.00%

iashik.com

Initial Budget Allocation of Munnariv

I Don't Have Any Money

I understand that for some of you reading this book, even raising $2,000 (₹50,000) might be a big challenge, let alone $7,000 (₹5,00,000). If you can only raise $100 (or ₹5,000) then allocate your money accordingly for food and travel. You might have to make the film in your backyard with your friends on your brother's phone that has a broken screen. Or you might have to do some job for 3 years like I did, save money and make the film for that. Go and read the story of how Robert Rodriguez sold his body to made his first film.

You can find ways to make it happen or excuses why you cannot make it happen.

The Dangers of Making Funding Requests to Friends

If you push too strong, and too often, they might stop taking your calls and start avoiding you in social situations. You could be putting your friendship at risk. Thankfully I was aware of the risk, as you are now. I never asked anyone more than twice. Most times only once; probably because of who I am.

In the end I might have heard 'no' from around 80 people, but what mattered were the 28 who said 'yes'. The amount each put in was entirely up to them, from as little as $13 (₹1,000) to a maximum of $700 (₹50,000).

> "It's not about your resources, it's about your resourcefulness." —
> Tony Robbins

Some requests were made in person, some through chat, some on call. We did not raise the money together, but over a year and half in various stages.

A Funding Story

Incidentally it all started with my grandmother out of the blue sending me a $700 (₹50,000) to go make my film, when I wasn't even thinking of making *Munnariv*. On top of that, my parents and my sister put in another $700 (₹50,000) each. I had $700 remaining after my travel and short film experiments over the years. I put that in. I found that this story of my family, especially that of my grandmother, chipping in to fund the venture gave others the encouragement to support too.

It Won't be Easy

But we made it happen. Have a story to tell. Let people know that they are helping you follow your dreams. Make them part of your journey. Call it 'our' film and not 'my' film.

Ironically, I realise now that by avoiding my fear of being rejected by two or three producers, I ended up being rejected by 100. Thankfully they were all my friends and family members. And I believe it helped develop my rejection muscles. Having made an 80 minutes feature film on a mobile phone, with few friends in my bedroom, I now have the confidence, and work to prove, that we can do it.

* * *

Making It Happen

If you have done all these steps:

- you have decided filmmaking is your path,
- learned the ins and outs of filmmaking,

- made short films, taken action towards your goals,
- worked on others' sets,
- built connections,
- written a script and
- raised enough money from your friends and family or a producer,

you are now ready to make your low budget film happen. Briefly let's look at what lies ahead.

Preproduction

The most important phase of making a low budget film is not the production, but the preproduction. It is going to affect everything about your film. The planning, budgeting and its execution can determine if you will end up with a completed film or one that you are still waiting for funds to complete. You absolutely need to complete the following:

- Script
- Breakdown of the script to the minutest detail
- Shot division or storyboard
- Locations
- Gear
- Props and costumes if any

Production

With a limited budget you are of course not going to be shooting for months and months; unless it's a film you are doing on the weekends. The exact number will depend on the script. Generally 12 to 21 days shoot is a sweet spot. You will have to take breaks in between as everyone would be doing multiple roles.

We shot *Munnariv* on an iPhone SE. We either used locations we already had access to, or we secured them for free. I had rewritten the script to let us shoot a major chunk of the film in my bedroom and places at a walkable distance from my house. All the actors used their own costumes. We had our maid cook delicious food (the most important aspect to keep morale up in a low budget film production).

Postproduction

This was one phase where I was scared if I would drop the ball. Therefore I had put aside enough money to get us through, right from preproduction. The following have to be locked in postproduction:

- Picture
- Music
- Sound
- Color

One of the actors in the *Munnariv* had worked earlier as an editor. He edited the whole film. A friend who was supposed to do the music skipped on us at the last minute. We will look at how you can have music in your film even without a composer and so on. I hope you now have the confidence to make your debut low budget film. In the following chapters we will explore in detail how you can execute it and finally market and sell your film. If we can do it, so can you.

* * *

3

Preproduction of an Indian Indie Film

Of all the phases of making a film, when it comes to a low budget film, the preproduction work done can make or break the whole project.

> *"If you want to just make a good movie, if you don't enjoy every step and become a master of each little moment, then you shouldn't be doing it."—Richard Linklater*

Let's look at some of the vital things you need before going into production and some softwares and tips to help you save time and money.

Script

What is a good story, how to craft one is a topic far beyond what any one book can teach you. Give what you've written to others and listen to them. If you are willing to listen and improve, even the common man outside will give you a piece of his mind on what they did not like in your story. Ask them why they feel what they feel. Most often they wanted/expected something that the story failed to deliver. It is your job to figure out where it failed and what you need to fix it. Ignore any specific instructions anyone has on what you need to change.

As you near production the practicality of visualising what you have written starts hitting you. At each of those challenges the two options you have is to rewrite around that obstacle or pour money to demolish it. You know what the solution is. Nonetheless have a fully bound script. Which is not to say you cannot make changes. You definitely should. But when you have a clearly written down script, with every scene, action and dialogue needed to convey the story, you are good to start preproduction.

Team

Choose wisely. A debut feature film is itself a big challenge. You want around you people whom you trust, respect, enjoy being around with and can get the job done. The same applies vice versa too.

Choose actors who are actors. They are the face of your film. Everyone knows when they see poor acting and it pulls the audience out of the film. Every effort you take will be seen reflected through their performance. The team you bring together in preproduction will be your legs, arms, tooth and nail in production.

Breakdown

You might read a line in the script that runs something like, he eats the rice. Is he eating with his hand, a spoon, a fork? Is it a wooden spoon or a plastic one? If he eating from a plate or some delivery packaging? Does any of this have to be in a certain color scheme?This is what an AD does while breaking down. He/she discusses with the director and figures out such minute details and notes it down.

Though breaking down of a script is the job of an AD, because of the budget, you or the director themselves might probably have to do it.

Breakdown the script to the minutest detail[3]. This is what you will be relying on to organise everything each day of the shoot.

Shot Division or Storyboard

The next step in prepping for the shoot is to have each scene broken down to its shots. How a scene is covered is how each director makes his/her mark. You can do this through a shot list or storyboards, whichever is comfortable to you. I draw stick figure storyboards.

Locations

We shot *Munnariv* in my bedroom. Use locations you already have access to. Your house, your parents' house, your ancestral house, your friend's farm, the gym you go to daily and so on. Get public locations for free, such as shops, malls, temples, parks and so on. If your ideal location is not available for free, go to the next one, and the one after. You can always find someone who will let you use their location for free. At times you can bargain with an exterior shot of the place, a shot of the actor buying something from their shop and so on.

Scheduling

If possible, shoot sequentially. It is easier for continuity and for actors. If you had rewritten the script as we discussed previously you probably have only few locations. Get those locations as close by as possible. Schedule in a day locations that are closest. Travelling from one location to another is tiring for everyone. Almost all of our locations, besides my

---

[3] One of the most succinct videos on script breakdowns that I have seen https://youtu.be/IMep2s_T89c

bedroom, were at most a 5 minutes drive from the house.

Scheduling is a game. One you only get good at with practice. Each production is different and so there is no one formula. If you have a talented and experienced AD it will be easier.

Gear

Use what you own and what your connections have. Spend as little as possible to get what you need to the editing table. It goes without saying, collect and test all the gear during preproduction. We shot a whole short film on the same mobile phone before going on set for the feature. Even then there were hiccups.

Props and Costumes

It depends on what the script demands and what you have. You would have identified these when you did the script breakdown. Again use as much as what you have, or what the crew has. Check with your friends and funders if they have what you are looking for. If none has, then buy. Even then try buying used ones or seconds, or renting if it is cheaper.

Budget

Have the money ready, in hand or in account, to whatever your schedule demands. Always have the money for everyone's food. You want an inspired and motivated crew. Some things will need more money, some less. Be prepared to reallocate your budget on the fly.

"Whatever story you want to tell, tell it at the right size". —Richard Linklater

Hope this gives you a starting idea of everything you need to do in preproduction. Once you know what you are doing like the back of your hand, you are ready to go[4]. Let us now look at some softwares that can assist you.

* * *

Celtx, Your Best Friend for Preproduction

If there is one piece of software that I have used over and over in my filmmaking career so far, it is Celtx. I'm not talking about the ridiculously priced cloud version, but the old, free desktop client. Even though all updates stopped in 2013 and Apple's 2019 Catalina update made it no longer usable on Macs, it is still one of the best free softwares out there for planning your film.

It is important to stay organised. A feature film production is a beast. Even if you are just making one with your friends in your backyard, it still needs a lot of things to come to together to put your vision on screen. Especially when you are working within a limited budget, you have a very low margin for error.

If a scene scheduled for tomorrow needs a certain property then you have to have it ready the previous day itself. You do not have the luxury of coming to set, finding out that you need certain pro and rush to a store. Celtx's old free desktop software can help you organise everything your film needs, from scriptwriting till the day you wrap the shoot.

---

[4] The blog noamkroll.com is a good resource on additional information on micro budget filmmaking.

Planning a Shoot with Celtx

An AD can breakdown the script to the minutest detail and tag it in Celtx. These are mapped to each scene and hence if a scene is reordered later, all the painstaking efforts of the AD are carried along with it. Celtx then lets you print out a breakdown sheet that has everything you so meticulously tagged.

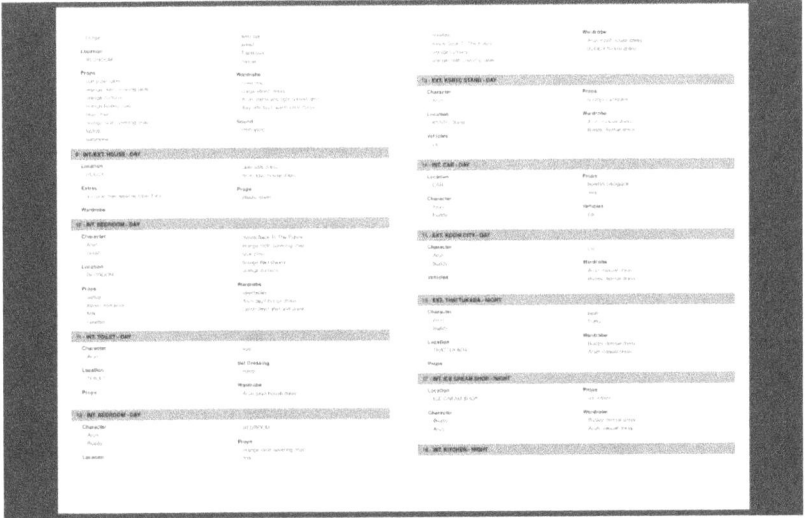

A Script Breakdown Sheet From Celtx

Later while scheduling you drag scenes into a calendar. After you've done that Celtx can provide you with one of the most useful reports you can have; a sheet with every element you need for each day of the shoot.

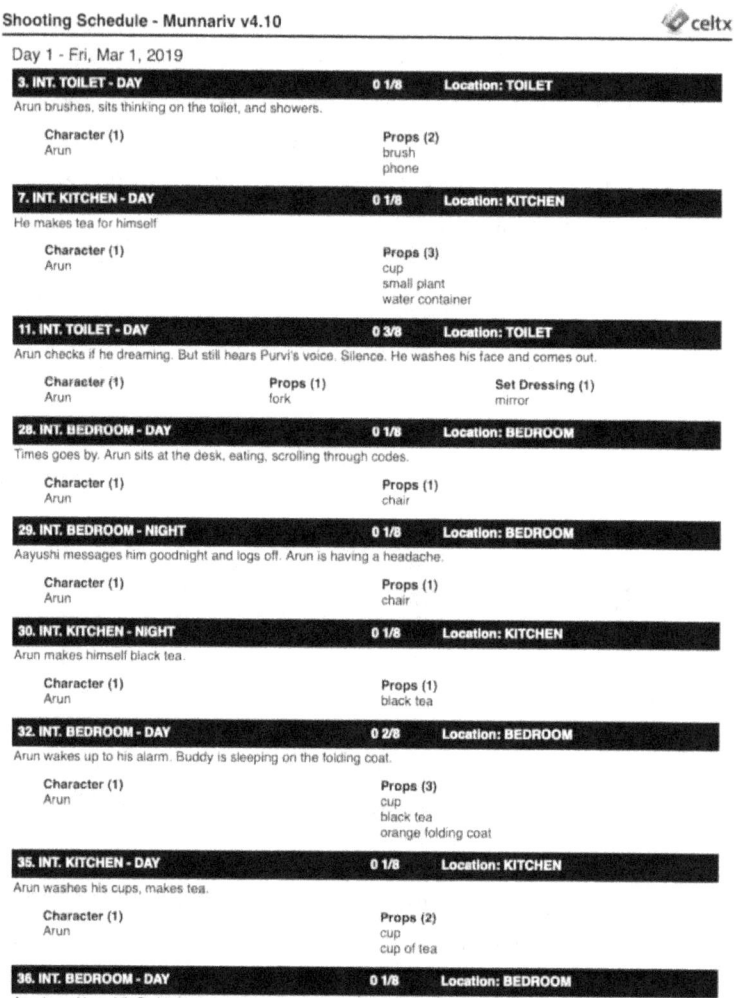

Day 1 - Fri, Mar 1, 2019

3. INT. TOILET - DAY   0 1/8   **Location: TOILET**

Arun brushes, sits thinking on the toilet, and showers.

Character (1)	Props (2)
Arun	brush
	phone

7. INT. KITCHEN - DAY   0 1/8   **Location: KITCHEN**

He makes tea for himself

Character (1)	Props (3)
Arun	cup
	small plant
	water container

11. INT. TOILET - DAY   0 3/8   **Location: TOILET**

Arun checks if he dreaming. But still hears Purvi's voice. Silence. He washes his face and comes out.

Character (1)	Props (1)	Set Dressing (1)
Arun	fork	mirror

28. INT. BEDROOM - DAY   0 1/8   **Location: BEDROOM**

Times goes by. Arun sits at the desk, eating, scrolling through codes.

Character (1)	Props (1)
Arun	chair

29. INT. BEDROOM - NIGHT   0 1/8   **Location: BEDROOM**

Aayushi messages him goodnight and logs off. Arun is having a headache.

Character (1)	Props (1)
Arun	chair

30. INT. KITCHEN - NIGHT   0 1/8   **Location: KITCHEN**

Arun makes himself black tea.

Character (1)	Props (1)
Arun	black tea

32. INT. BEDROOM - DAY   0 2/8   **Location: BEDROOM**

Arun wakes up to his alarm. Buddy is sleeping on the folding coat.

Character (1)	Props (3)
Arun	cup
	black tea
	orange folding coat

35. INT. KITCHEN - DAY   0 1/8   **Location: KITCHEN**

Arun washes his cups, makes tea.

Character (1)	Props (2)
Arun	cup
	cup of tea

36. INT. BEDROOM - DAY   0 1/8   **Location: BEDROOM**

Arun is working while Buddy leaves.

A Schedule Report Exported From Celtx

This might not seem like much, but remember that a shoot never happens sequentially. In a day's shoot you might need 10 different clothes for an actor alone. You need to know in advance what those are going to be so that you have time to get it washed, ironed and ready for shoot.

Con of Using Celtx

Besides being of no use in postproduction, the only disadvantage that I have ever faced with the old free desktop software of Celtx is that it does not support regional languages. This is major problem for us Indians. We have 22 working film industries in 22 different regional languages. You can use the software to write in regional languages. But if you want to export anything as a PDF, all you will get are files with boxes.

It is not that they cannot support, but they want you to use their paid version and hence the restriction. We work around that by not exporting as PDF files. But instead we use the software's print command and then save as a PDF. *Jugaad!*

Another way of getting around is to type the regional language using English alphabets, the many variants of *Hinglish*, *Manglish* and so on. It will look unprofessional. But who cares as long as everyone on your team is okay with it. For Munnairv I wrote all the action lines in English, while all the dialogues were in *Manglish* (Malayalam written in English).

Celtx's Ridiculously Priced Online Version

Time on set is expensive. Whatever you can do to make sure that you are as prepared as you can be, is saving you a lot of money. Which could be why you might want to look into paid alternatives.

Celtx's cloud version lets you write your script for free. It supports regional languages. But anything outside of that—breakdown, scheduling, and so on—you need to pay a hefty subscription fee of over $230 (₹17,000), for just one person to use it for one year. But the saddest thing is that the hefty fee doesn't even let everybody on your team use it. Every film would have around 2 or 4 Assistant Directors, and at the least take around a year or two to go from scripting to the completion of production. That puts the price over $21,000 (₹16,00,000)!

I don't see how that pricing is justified whatsoever. You can of course get one subscription, share the account, and all of that. We did that in a film that I was an AD for. It was what enabled me to get the job done as efficiently as I did. Even if it were a big budget production or a production house with multiple projects running simultaneously, I'd recommend something else.

StudioBinder – A Better Paid Alternative

I have only heard of and not used StudioBinder. For 6 assistant directors to use StudioBinder, with unlimited projects (mind you, Celtx's $230 fee lets you create only 30 projects) for 2 years it costs only $700 (₹50,000). That pricing is understandable and reasonable.

Note:All prices and suggestions are as of writing this book and are subject to change.

It saddens me to see the creators of one of my favourite filmmaking apps loose sight of what they had. They might have some plans that I cannot see. Anyway I pray for the best to them. Meanwhile for all of us filmmakers the old Celtx desktop client will do everything you need to get your film in the can. It is free. Download now and make your film happen.

* * *

Storyboarder, An Outstanding Storyboarding Software

If you want to create storyboards and have not heard of Storyboarder, then you are in for a treat. Storyboarder is a software for Mac and Windows that lets you create storyboards. It is free and it is an awesome piece of software.

  If you already have a script written, you can find lots of free softwares to turn your script into the open source Fountain format that Story-boarder uses. You can use the software without any script attached as well, just so you know.

Shot Generator

For someone like me who has no sketching skills, one of the biggest features was something called a Short Generator. You can select from drop-downs exactly what you need—man/women, close up/wide, running/sitting, night/day, above/side lit and lots more—and get a reference image.

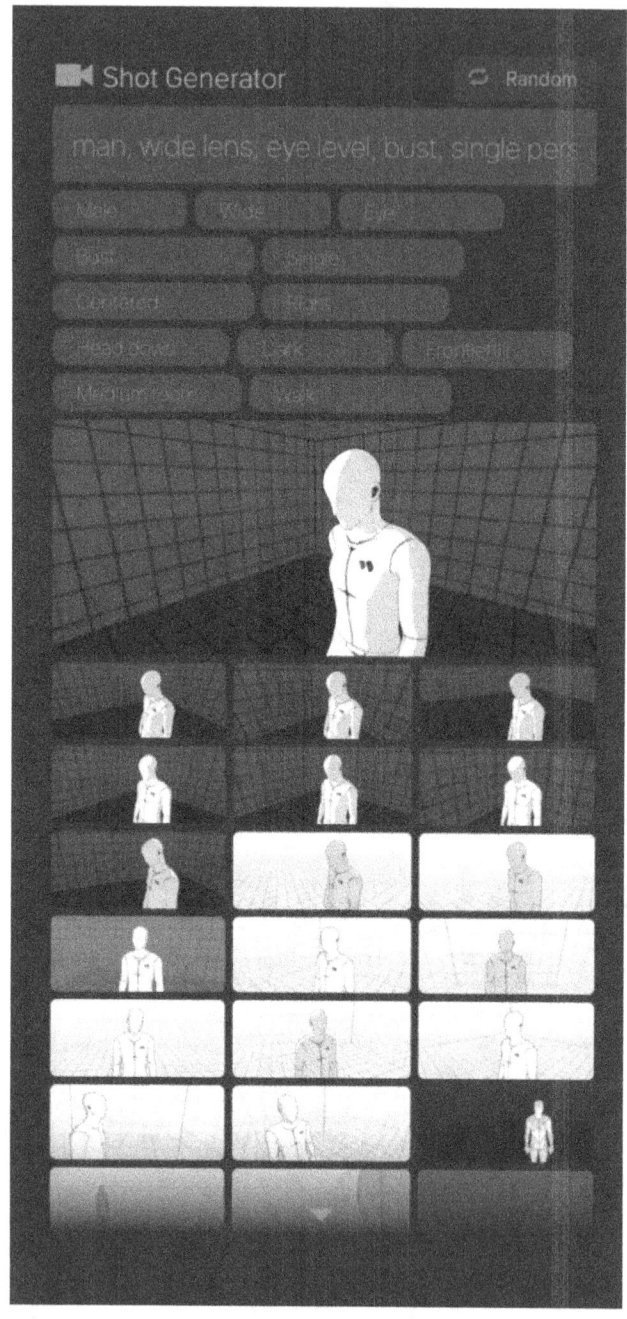

Shot Generator in Storyboarder

Once you have found what you are looking for, in one click this reference shot gets imported into the board. You can then easily trace an outline (or use the reference itself). If you are someone who can sketch, the advantage is that these reside only in something called a 'Light Layer'. You can adjust its opacity as needed and perfect your drawing on top of it. You can also import an external image into the Light Layer for tracing.

Integration with Photoshop

Most design artists work on Adobe's Photoshop. They are more used to its tools. Hence it is understandable if they are hesitant to use this new software. But as you have guessed from the subheading, Storyboarder integrates with Photoshop. All the layers from Storyboarder are retained when imported into Photoshop. Including the reference layer you might have added. In case you draw using a PSD editor other than Photoshop, you can edit the boards in that as well.

Why Use Storyboarder At All?

If you are anyway going to be drawing in Photoshop, you might be wondering this. A very good question. Let me tell you why; Organisation.

When I am writing, I want to be writing. I don't want to be thinking about versioning or formatting. I want to concentrate on the words. Similarly when you are sketching, you don't want to be thinking of saving the files, naming them based on scenes, using conventions of the stage you are in and so on. If free flowing creativity is a left brain activity, let's call organisation a right brain activity. When you are doing one, you do not want to be thinking of the other. Else it is a recipe for getting stuck and curbing your flow.

If you are using Storyboarder, it takes care of organisation. It saves automatically. All boards are linked to the scenes in the script. You can rearrange or reorder the boards, or scenes and all the boards will be reorganised accordingly. No going back through files and renaming all of them. Which can make a lot of difference in your flow of creativity and the number of iterations you might want to go through.

Sketching For People Who Want to Use Hands

The features list this software offers keeps growing! Some artists like to sketch by hand. If you are one of them, then your needs are taken care of too. Once you have your project started, you can printout worksheets for each scene that has QR codes on them. Take them out with you, sketch on them, take a photo of the page and import it into Storyboarder. Every sketch you made will be imported into exactly that scene, with each board cut out and placed automatically. Beautiful! What more can I say! These sketches are placed again in the reference layer, if you wish to enhance it later.

An Active Storyboarder Users Group on Facebook

Besides the inspiring efforts in developing this piece of software, another wonderful thing is the active Facebook group of Storyboarder users. The creators of the software moderate the group and use it to collect feedback and brainstorm new ideas and features for the software. Moreover from a user perspective, if you are facing a problem using Storyboarder, posting it there brings in the collective knowledge of all the users and might help you solve it faster. This is not to say you will always get a solution, but the likelihood is higher than searching for it somewhere else.

Other Promising Features

There are even more? Yes! Some of the features that I am yet to make use of, but tickles the techie fan boy in me:

- Using smartphone as a controlling device to articulate the reference models
- Virtual Reality

And they keep figuring out what users need and adding it month after month. How is this software even free!

Cons of Storyboarder

It is only in the process of becoming a fully fleshed out storyboarding software. It has its bugs, crashes at times, the import to Photoshop might not always have the layers and so on.

The only reason I am not recommending it to every production is because there is no option to export the boards of an entire script as a PDF in one go, as of writing this. You have to go to each scene and export it one after the other. If it a short film that should not be a problem. But unlike a short film, most feature films have over a hundred scenes.

It is tedious in itself to draw hundreds, if not thousands, of boards. Exporting should not be so. Hence I have been hesitant to use it for a feature so far. I had raised the concern in the Facebook Group some time back. As I was updating the software to write this article, it showed a 'Custom PDF Exports' in its Coming Soon features list. Hopefully it addresses this.

Still I Recommend Storyboarder

For truly understanding the pain points of filmmakers and making a software that solves it, it is an outstanding piece of storyboarding software. And on top of that giving it out for free, humbled!

For years people said you should write scripts if you did not have the resources to pull together a feature. Now not only can you write the script of the film, but you can visualise every frame of it in detail. Imagine the confidence you might inspire in a producer when you approach them with a fully bound fantabulous script and a detailed storyboard.

Go to wonderunit.com/storyboarder, download now and go make your films happen.

* * *

4

Production of an Indian Indie Film

A multitude of things are happening on set simultaneously. It is something that you learn best by doing. The variables are so far and wide (also why it will not immediately be overthrown by a software).

What Happens During Production

I know people who love being on set more than anything. It is not my favourite part of the filmmaking process. To me it is something I dread on the days leading to it, chaotic and stressful in the beginning, a wonderful time with fun people in the middle, relieved towards the end, and dearly missed soon afterwards.

I am not a morning person. But every day of a shoot you end up waking early. Yes I love filmmaking, storytelling is my passion. I look forward to each day's challenges and love what I get to do. Even then the act of having to leave my bed, those initial moments, are not my favourite.

What happens on set varies with the role one plays in it. To anyone standing outside and watching, it looks like a lot of people sitting around, talking, some running, basically doing nothing. To anyone in it, it is anything but.

To an assistant director, it is managing people who are late. To an actor it is waiting for the set to be ready. To a makeup man it is talking. To a producer it is running out of time. To a cameraman it is the stray light hitting the wall. To a sound recordist it is the barking dog that no one cares about but them. To a director it is to get the perfect take. To the extras it is the food.

Finding Solutions to Problems

That is what actually happens on set. Every minute of every hour of every shoot day is another problem to be solved. The better you are prepared with the work you did in preproduction, the easier it is to find solutions during production. It all starts with the script. Every solution is about practically bringing it to life with available resources. Get onto be on as many sets as possible. It could be your own low budget films, or someone else's.

* * *

Mobile Filmmaking

As you already know, our debut film was shot entirely on an iPhone SE. For fellow aspiring filmmakers, mobile filmmaking is now opening up possibilities that filmmakers of the yesteryears could not even dream of. Even then mobile filmmaking can be frightening. Let us look in detail at everything we learnt in our journey, so that we save you some pain.

Why iPhone Over Other Smartphones?

Having used Apple computers for some years now, I might be becoming a fan boy. But it was not the reason. Even the app we used to shoot the film, FiLMiC Pro, was available on both iOs and Android Operating Systems (OS). We used an iPhone purely to reduce the number of unknowns.

With Android phones, the OS is developed by one firm, while its hardware is designed by another, and apps by a third party. For third party developers, testing their apps on all the countless android phone models being manufactured by hundreds of companies is impossible.

Whereas Apple builds its own software and hardware of their phones. Moreover only a handful of models exist at any time. So when a third party app developer claims that their app will work on a particular iPhone, we can know with a better certainty that it will work, reducing the risk of it disturbing the filming.

Lenses and Hardware

Besides the software we also needed lenses and attachments to enhance the visuals. We wanted to go with something that has already been tested and known to work. Hence we went with the same gear that was used previously, such as in the films *Tangerine* and *High Flying Bird*.

Shooting a whole feature on a mobile brings with itself a lot of unknowns. As far as possible we wanted to reduce the known risk factors. Hence choosing to shoot on a tried and tested device and additional hardware was a logical decision to ensure we could achieve a finished product.

Why iPhone SE?

Choosing the iPhone SE over other iPhone models was fairly easy. It was based on the following two needs:

- 4K footage We had decided that the final film would be in 1080p. Hence shooting in 4K resolution would let us zoom in on shots in the edit, create artificial dolly/track shots and so on as needed.
- Keep expenses low This was fairly obvious. iPhone SE was the cheapest iPhone that could shoot 4K. Even then we did not have the resources to buy a new one. So we brought a second hand phone off eBay, while eBay was still active in India.

Mobile Filmmaking Gear We Used in Munnariv

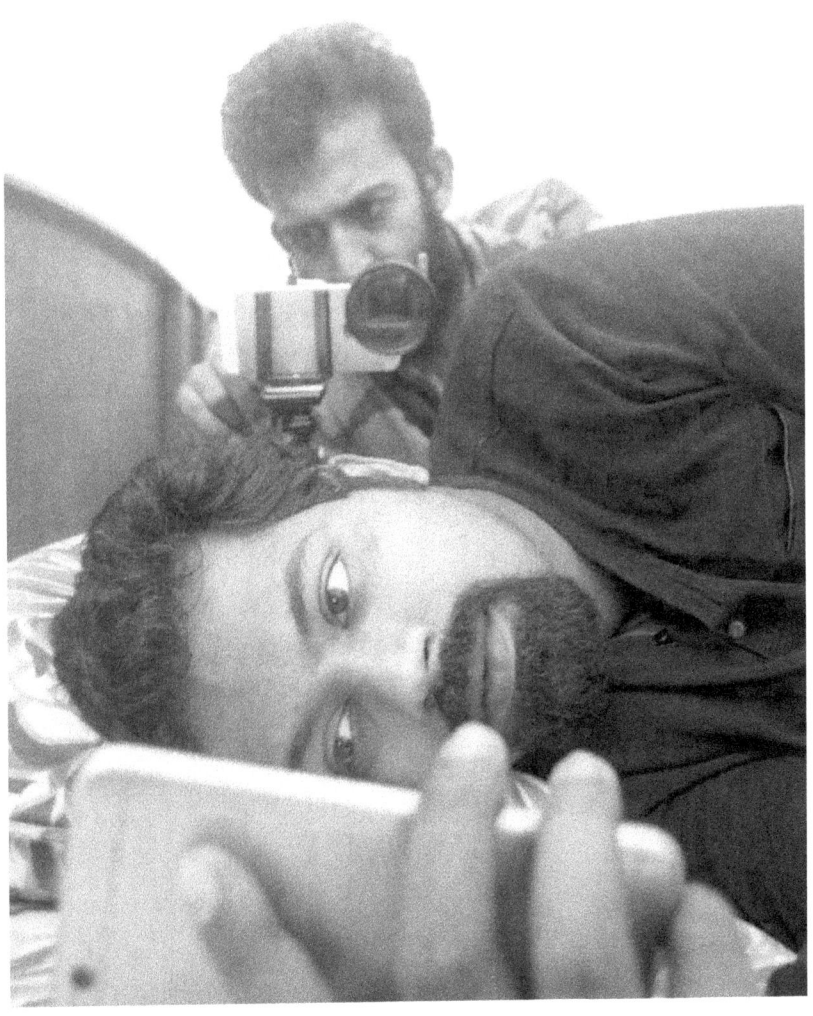

Shooting Handheld

The mobile filmmaking gear we used in detail are as follows:

1. Two iPhone SE
2. Moondog Labs 1.33X Anamorphic Lens – for iPhone 5/5S and iPhone SE
3. Moondog Labs 52mm Filter Mount – for Clamp-on Anamorphic Lenses
4. Hoya 52 mm Polariser Filter
5. Tiffen 52 mm to 58 mm Step-Up Adapter
6. Tiffen 58DVFMK3 58 mm DV Film Look Filter Kit 3
7. Solar power bank by Poweradd
8. Cheap phone holder for the tripod
9. Sonia Pro 777 Tripod (that is designed to carry upto 10 kg; the irony!)

Diffusion Filters on an iPhone

As the film progressed, we wanted the visuals of *Munnariv* to convey a sense of the protagonist's increasing confusion and unclarity. One way of achieving this in-camera was to use diffusion filters like Black Pro Mist Filter and so on. Diffusion filters are a secret tool of the olden day cinematographers. They were regularly used in film photography as well as in early digital cinematography, but lost somewhere in the DSLR revolution. It lets you add degrees of softness to the visuals as you need.

Though we extensively searched for people who might have previously used diffusion filters on an iPhone, we couldn't find anything anywhere online. Hence we had to take the risk on ourselves. We bought the Tiffen DV Film Look Filter Kit from Amazon.

Testing the Mobile Filmmaking Gear

There weren't many experienced people around to whom we could discuss mobile filmmaking. Hence we had to become the experts ourselves. Following the principles of low budget filmmaking, once we had all the gear we needed, we made two test short films. Yes, two! Such intensive testing of all the mobile filmmaking gear ahead of jumping into the feature film helped us identify some of the advantages and disadvantages early on.

Advantages of Mobile Filmmaking

While going through the process and now reminiscing about it, the following are some of the advantages we see on shooting on an iPhone, or any phone for that matter:

- It is **unobtrusive**. Many a time we would forget that there was a camera rolling. To outsiders it looked like some random kids fooling around on their phone.
- The sheer **outrageousness** of how the whole thing sounds! And the bewilderment we see when we finally tell someone that we made a whole film on device in their pockets.
- Almost every **accessory is cheaper**. For example, a gimbal, anamorphic lens, tripod, crane, filters, all of these cost less than the same you would need for an SLR or a cinema camera.
- Hopefully **inspire** and remind other filmmakers that we live in a time unlike any other in history where we can indeed go out and make a film.

Disadvantages of Mobile Filmmaking

The following are some of the disadvantages of mobile filmmaking:

- **Heat**! The normal iPhone camera shoots at a bitrate of 50 Mbps. Using FiLMiC Pro we doubled it to have more date in post production. On top of that we were charging the phone while shooting. This frequently heated it up the phone and made it unresponsive. We could not start or stop the recording and lost a lot of takes. The tropical climate of Kerala at the start of summer did not help either. We ended up having a lot of icepacks.

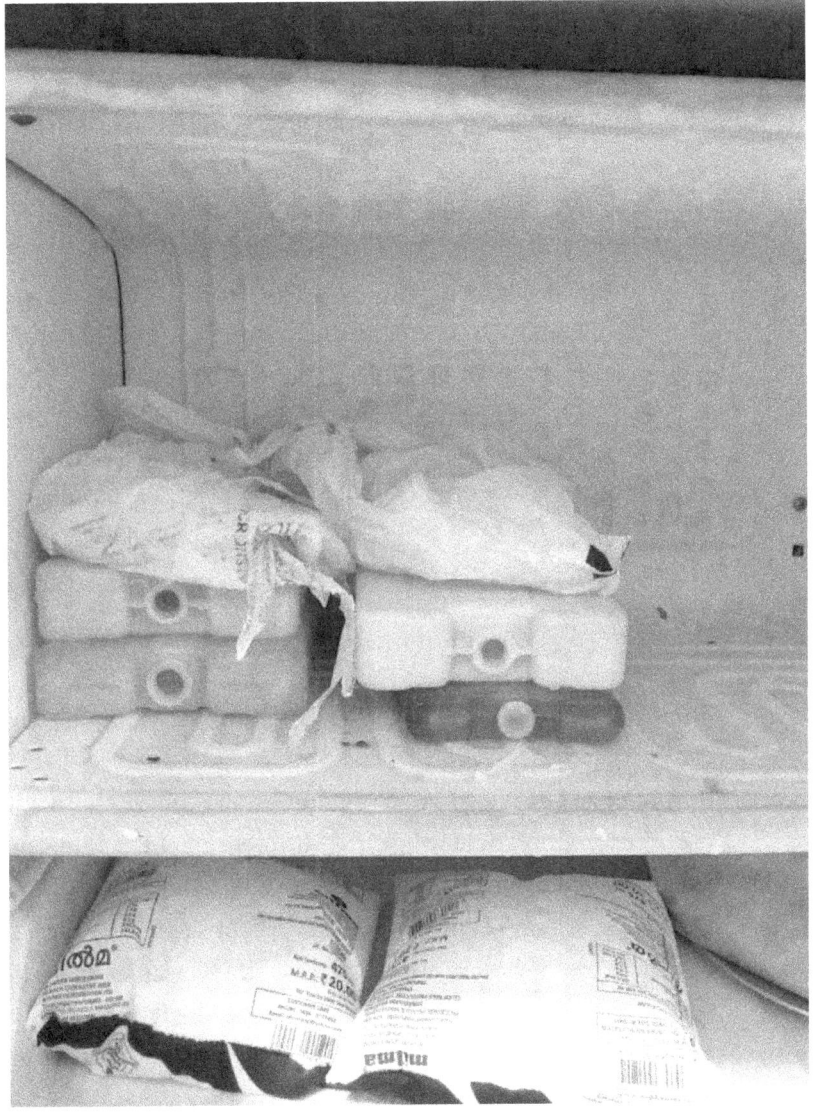

- Inability to judge if a shot is in **focus**. On the tiny screen everything looks sharp. But when we pulled the footage into a laptop, some of the shots were not so.
- **Mid take exposure change**. This is something many filmmakers

too have complained about. Even when the exposure was locked, in the middle of some takes the exposure would change abruptly. There is nothing you can do about it, but try to correct it somehow in post production (extremely time consuming).

- The iPhone SE records videos using 8 bits of data. Most phones do. Video files using an **8 bit codec** have limited information compared to that using a 10 bit codec. Having used FiLMiC Pro at high bitrates, we did have a better flexibility with the footage during color grading. But if you are planning to push and pull the footage a lot, the 8 bit file does not leave much room. It breaks up soon and results in banding.

These were some of the advantages and disadvantages of mobile film-making as we experienced it.

Why we Bought a Second iPhone

The heating up of the phone was a major problem. We would have to stop the shoot and wait for it to cool down. As we had the ice packs, we got the phone to cool down in 3 or 4 minutes. But during those unexpected breaks everyone would drift into a different mood and it would take at least 10 minutes to get everyone focused back on the shoot.

Our first schedule was for 5 days. As soon as we wrapped we had to make a choice, whether to pay for a second iPhone, or pay with slower shoots and hence a longer schedule. We decided to spend money. The anamorphic lens we had would not fit any other model but an iPhone SE. We went to local shops looking for another used iPhone SE.

We found one, that too with a larger storage of 64 GB. The first had 16 GB and gave only around 10 GB of usable storage. This was also adding to unexpected delay as we constantly had to offload footage. The second 64 GB model cost us more than the first one. We didn't have time to check and order online either. But this money spent saved us a lot of time and energy everyday for the rest of the shoot. This is also why breaks are important to have planned in advance, especially for low budget films.

* * *

Schedule Breaks in an Indie Production

In some regional Indian film industries, schedule breaks are not the norm. With even some big budget productions the shoots are scheduled non-stop for 30 to 40 days.

I come from a more streamlined workspace of IT where both Saturdays and Sundays are off. So to me that is madness. Schedule breaks are a luxury that big budget productions might not be able to afford. While making your debut low budget film, not only can you afford breaks, but it is an advantage that you must make use of.

Breaks Add Creativity

In a full scale production each department has its own personnel. While in a low budget film, you and everyone in your team are going to be doing multiple roles simultaneously. For *Munnariv*, the 10 people on set did everything from acting to lights, sets and costumes. Doing this continuously for a stretch of time is taxing. Doing any kind of work for 12 hours a day continuously for 10 or 12 days is draining.

Your crew might be ready to push themselves for you. But when the body is tired, the brain shuts off. It does not have enough resources to come up with solutions. You are always facing challenges when on set. The creativity with which you solve those challenges is the creativity you see on screen. If you did your job properly in preproduction, then a lot of those decisions would have been made earlier, when you had time

73

to think and decided clearly.

Breaks Reduce Expenses

Besides giving you the time to recharge, breaks give you time to analyse what you have made so far. If you are yourself the editor, or if you have someone editing, during the breaks you can quickly put together an assembly cut and see what you have shot, as opposed to the film you see in your head.

Even when there are spot editors, or an editor editing in parallel, with long productions, the director gets to see what he/she has shot only after the shoot has wrapped. In case they missed something, or if in the edit they feel that an additional pickup shot can enhance the story, then they have to reassemble the whole team and plan a reshoot.

At times one additional shot of an actor looking this way or that way can make the edit flow smoother. It can keep the audience engaged. Though there are always ways to work around something, when you know this while you are in production, it is a simple matter to capture it. It is no extra effort for anyone.

Greasing The Engine

Besides missed shots, there are always other problems coming up during production, such as the unexpected issue we faced with the iPhone heating up in our tropical climate. There could be problems with an actor's availability, a location might have fallen off at the last minute, you might have missed a scene and so on.

When the production is running it is like a train at full speed. Halting at a station lets you check in on the brakes, the engines, the wheels. A throwaway act like greasing a joint might not seem like much. But if such corrections are not done on time, the whole train can get derailed.

You might have to recast an actor, replace a torn dress, reschedule and so on. Breaks give you time to regroup and solve issues; to take a breather from the rolling high speed train and think clearly. Other problems will rise again as the schedule restarts. You know you can tackle them when you have breaks planned in advance.

Even if it is just a two days break, it lets you rest, solve problems, and gets you ready to be back on set. Remember, a finished product is better than no product. Taking breaks is a luxury that even big budget productions can't afford, but you can. Use it well.

* * *

Great Food Motivation

If there is one thing that can keep everyone going while making your low budget film, it is tasty food on set. Yes it might seem silly, but it is also the truth.

You might be making one of the most wonderful films that the world has ever seen. The script might be an inspiring and heart touching one that every single person in the crew loved. But when it is shoot day number 12 or 21, when they have been pushing through the grind for so many days, all of the non immediate pleasures stop being a reason to get out of the bed again.

Why It Matters More For a Low Budget Film

If you are making a normal budget film, everyone is getting paid in full. You'd be working with professionals who do this day in and day out. With them you do not have to worry so much about keeping them motivated. Of course you can't completely ignore the team's pulse either.

But because you are making a passion project, a low budget film with your friends or colleagues, everyone is chipping in their time to help you achieve your dream. They could be elsewhere and earning a lot more than what you'd be paying them. In return it is important that you take care of them in all ways, as best as you can. Having great food on set every day is the most tangible way you can do that.

Food On Set of Munnariv

For food on set of our debut film we spent around $7 (₹500) per person per day. Which is actually a lot more than a normal budget feature film here in Kerala, India. There are Ad shoots that spend $14 (₹1,000) per person per day. But those shoots barely last few days, have a different purpose, and so cannot be compared to a feature film set.

We had scheduled every shoot day centred around my house. Hence our house maid herself did the cooking, for an additional fee. She is an incredible cook by the way. My parents made everyday's breakfasts, as the maid would not reach before that. We had all varieties of dishes, from veg to non-veg, from South Indian to North Indian. Everyone served themselves, and washed their own plates. This avoided the need for an additional hand.

Scheduling Food On Set

The food on set every day looked something like this:

- As soon as everyone arrived, a cup of steaming hot tea
- Soon followed by breakfast with another cup of tea (the items kept changing everyday, almost all Kerala breakfast dishes were served)
- After the shoot had been going on for some time, around 10 or 11 AM, a glass of lime juice and biscuits as refreshment

- Around noon, lunch was served (Kerala meals with fish curry, chicken/fish fry or any other speciality dish and a sweet)
- Around 4 PM, a cup of tea with a Kerala snack (at times made at home, else brought from a really good store nearby)
- Once the shoot wrapped, around 8 or 9 PM, dinner was served (which could be chapatti or fried rice with beef/chicken curry, or Kerala meals and so on)

Besides these, there were snacks all around the house for anyone to have at any time they liked. Timely and tasty food on set every day shows the crew that you care for their wellbeing. When they feel taken care of, they take care of your production. Cut costs wherever you can, but spend well on food. On a low budget film set you might not be paying your crew in kind, but make sure you pay them in kindness, generously.

* * *

5

Postproduction of an Indian Indie Film

Starting a project is easy. You are inspired, the future looks bright, there are lots of people around to help you. By the time you have gone through the planning and hectic production days to reach postproduction, there is no energy left. There is no one around. Just you and a system. You might have heard of 'Development Hell'. For low budget films, Postproduction Hell is just as real. Rightfully this is one phase you should be cautious of. Especially about having enough money to pull through.

Reallocating Budget

Even if you had budgeted properly in preproduction and did everything to run the production within it, you would still have eaten into some of your postproduction budget. When you have run out of motivation, raising funds can be a lot more difficult. Hence I repeat again, work diligently in preproduction. Figure out everything that your specific film would need in postproduction and accommodate its expenses beforehand.

What Happens in Postproduction

At a high level only the following needs to happen in postproduction:

- Assembly of the film
- Assembly of the sounds
- Coloring the visuals
- Delivering the final film

If you have done any kind of video work, this would be self evident. Even if not, there are infinite number of resources online that you can learn in depth about each of them. So let's talk about things that I learnt from my experience.

* * *

Working in Reels

If you have not worked in a feature film format before, then this is something you need to be aware of. One thing different in the postproduction of a feature film, from that of shorts, is that everything happens in reels. Reels are nothing but your film split into pieces, each of a duration between 15 to 18 minutes.

The editor creates these reels. Each reel will have a one frame beep at the beginning and end. They hand it over to the other departments. The sounds are created and mixed reel by reel, while at the same time color grading is done, again reel by reel. The editor later combines the new visuals and sounds, synched with the one frame beeps, and is exported again, reel by reel.

79

Why Reels?

When I questioned why this was so, what I was told was that it was easier on the machines to process 15/18 minute projects than one that was an hour or two long. It reduced the chances of a system crash. And in case a crash happens, you don't lose everything, but maybe only a 15 minute portion of the film. I don't know how true that is. Maybe it is dogma that is still being followed from the practices of the celluloid film world.

* * *

Using Sound Design to Tell Stories

Using sound design to tell stories is an integral element of filmmaking that I'm still only learning. To me personally the other elements of a film stand out more; like the story, characters, actors, cinematography, set design and so on. Probably because they are more in-your-face. I could not find citation to claim that 90% of all information entering the brain is visual. But there seems to proof[5] that more of our neurons are dedicated to vision than the other four senses combined. Whatever the case may be, vision seems to have a stronger hold on me than sound.

Why Sound Design Matters

Films have always had sound. Believe it or not, even the silent films had sound. They might not have had sounds as we define it, but they were always accompanied with a live orchestra. In fact, a lot of musicians lost their job when film reels started arriving with recorded music.

---

5   https://www.imagethink.net/true-or-false-vision-rules-the-brain/

Can you think of watching a film without sound? Try it. I have. But I was dissecting the film and wanted to focus on the visuals. If it is a bad film you won't understand anything. It would just be shots of people talking with the whole story told through dialogues. The reason why my ears get strained in theatres is because most of Malayalam commercial films are radio shows with pretty pictures.

> *"If it's a good movie, the sound could go off and the audience would still have a perfectly clear idea of what was going on." —* *Alfred Hitchcock*

The Particular Case of Alfred Hitchcock

That quote might seem contradictory to our topic of discussion, but do not be fooled by Hitchcock. For all filmmakers looking into storytelling through sound, he is a director of particular interest.

Hitchcock is one of those few directors that started their career in the silent film era and lived an illustrious one through the sound era. Of all his great films, there is one that is pertinent to sound. It is one of his early films that came in the middle of the transition to sound, *Blackmail* (1929). What is peculiar about *Blackmail* is that it is one of the most successful films to be made simultaneously as a silent film and as a talkie. A rarity now. If you can find copies of both versions, it is worth a study in comparison. It can help you understand some of the creative ways with which Hitchcock enhanced the same story using visuals and then by adding sounds to it.

How Hitchcock used Sound Design in Blackmail

The leading lady in the film accidentally stabs a man who was trying to rape her. She runs from the scene and is later near a dinning table. One of the characters siting at the table is holding a knife. Using a knife while having food is normal, but this knife reminds her of the knife she had used earlier to kill the man.

In the silent version, Hitchcock repeatedly cuts to a close shot of the knife, gleaming and turning menacingly under the light. It is intercut with her disturbed face. Whereas in the sound version, he beautifully uses the other character's voice to add to the leading lady's turmoil. Though what that character says is irrelevant to the story, they have beautifully crafted those ramblings to have a lot of 'knife' in it. And the brilliance of Hitchcock's sound design is that in the mix he made just those words of 'knife' stand out. On top of that he kept raising that character's pitch whenever the word 'knife' was said. What starts out as a subtle 'knife', or a 'knife!', towards the end becomes an almost unbearable impressionistic shriek of 'KNIFE!' 'KNIFE!'.

And this was Hitchcock's first film with sound. His later films do not have silent versions and its sound design becomes such an integral part of it that is harder to dissect.

How Sound Design Works

Sound works at the subconscious level, whereas visuals stand out more as they are right in front of us. It is the sound that creates the not-so-tangible world of the film. Good sound design is what helps us immerse ourselves in the story. It is difficult to explain in words how sounds can heavily influence storytelling. I would suggest you to watch an analysis video of how sound designer Ben Burtt used sounds in Steven Spielberg's film *Munich*. The video is titled 'See With Your Ears: Spielberg And Sound

Design'[6].

What is Sound Design

Broadly speaking, sound design creates the auditory experience by using the following elements:

- Dialogue
- Music
- Foley
- Ambience
- Sound Mix

In the following pages we will look at each of these.

***

Dubbing or Sync Sound

In India, it's known as dubbing. Elsewhere it's called Automatic/Automated Dialogue Replacement (ADR) or Looping. It is the long process of recording each and every dialogue spoken by actors in a film. Synchronised sound, colloquially known as sync sound and more professionally called production audio, is the sound recorded from the actors while on set.

---

[6] See With Your Ears: Spielberg And Sound Design https://youtu.be/kavxsXhzD48

Dubbing And India

Majority of all Indian films are dubbed, while most other film industries use production audio. To them ADR is looked down upon. Though Indians have been embracing it recently we too have started looking down on dubbing. More and more films are now turning to use only production audio. I believe *Lagaan* was one of the first ones to be widely acclaimed.

"Is dubbing or sync sound better" is a question that has been raging for some time in the filmmaking community. I used to believe production audio was better. It captured the actor's performance at that moment. It would be exactly the sound that I, as the director, would have said okay to. But if you are making a low budget film, dubbing is the way to go. Here is why.

Time On Set is Expensive

If you are recording sound along with picture, then you need to have a person dedicated to do that. No questions there. Take my word for it.

You are set the first day. A take went well and you just called cut. That dedicated sound person you hired comes to you and tells you that a dog barked while the actor spoke and politely asks for a retake. They cannot use that take. It is like if an actor slipped during a take. You of course cannot correct that in post. So you go for that second take.

The camera moved perfectly as you hoped, the actors performed way better, you are happy you went for the second take and calls cut. The sound person comes and tells you a car honked while the actor spoke and asks for a retake. Of course they cannot correct that in post. So you convince the actor and team for another take. Everyone unwillingly goes for another take because you asked. The performance was not good in this one. So you call for another take. This time the camera lost focus on the actor while they moved. You call for another take, but now the actor's make up need retouching. Then you take another take. Thankfully everything came together for this take. You look at the sound guy. He tells you that a cow cried from the neighbour's house. Do you go for another take, or do you tell him we will dub it later?

Non-Ideal Locations

Finding a location required by the script, which is the best place for the visuals, silent enough to record clean audio, and is available for free is a difficult combination. If you have the time to do it, then by all means. Else you have to compromise one. Which then should you compromise on? We chose sound. Not because it is inferior to the other. Good quality sound is far more important than beautiful visuals. But we choose to dub the film later because we knew we had access to studios.

Accessibility to Recording Studios

As all Indian film industries have for years been dubbing, we have access to a lot of good quality recording studios for cheap. Not only film recording studios, but there are music recording studios as well. If you have seen *Gully Boy*, you might have seen a scene in which they go to a tiny studio in the middle of a ghetto. Such recording places, and even more affordable professional studios, can be found in every city in India. The cheapest one that I have heard of, doing professional quality work in Kochi, is around $ 7 (₹500) per hour. This includes everything related to recording (mixing charges are higher). On average a feature takes around 8 days to dub, working 8/9 hours a day, that comes to around $500 (₹35,000). We were cheapskate. We didn't do that either.

Setup a Home Dubbing Studio

We dubbed the whole film in my friend's bedroom.

My friend already had all required equipments from his father's shut down studio (remember making connections). We dubbed after his office hours, from 7 in the evening till 12 in the midnight, everyday for 2 months. As we did not have a sound proof studio, we had to stop every time an aeroplane went by or the crickets started. After all, time was what we had.

You either pay with money or with time, if you want to make a quality product.

In low budget filmmaking you are always compromising one thing for another. It is each of those decisions that you take that shapes the film you are making. As far as possible make choices keeping the audience in mind. Based on my resources, I knew for *Munnariv* dubbing was the cheaper option that offered the best auditory experience to the audience. What will yours be?

> *"Dialogue should simply be a sound among other sounds, just something that comes out of the mouths of people whose eyes tell the story in visual terms."* — *Alfred Hitchcock*

* * *

Music Without A Composer

While we were in the preproduction stages of *Munnariv* we had hired a composer to do its music. As postproduction was nearing completion without any warning he quit on us. Not delivering any music of course.

Being already late for a festival submission we had no time to find another composer. We were left with no option but to make music without a composer.

Royalty Free Music

The first thing that came to my mind, and one that I have made use of in my short films before, was finding royalty free music. I've often relied on websites like SoundCloud to find music that are licensed under Creative Common (CC) licenses. These are tracks that you can use for free. If you go this route, be sure to search for CC licence to use commercially. Only these can be sold along with your film.

Limitation

The downside is that there are a lot of sites with Royalty Free Music that are only average in quality. Just search and listen to some. You will hear what I mean. It is a lot to wade through. If you have the time and patience you can.

Artlist

The next option is to use a more curated website. The people composing music also need to make a living. Hence the good ones tend to put their music on websites that pay them some form of fee. Also we did not have time to surf though a lot of junk. Hence this was the route we chose to go with for *Munnariv*, in particular the website artlist.io. One of the most useful features of Artlist is their search filter. You can search by the mood, theme, genre or any instruments you particularly need.

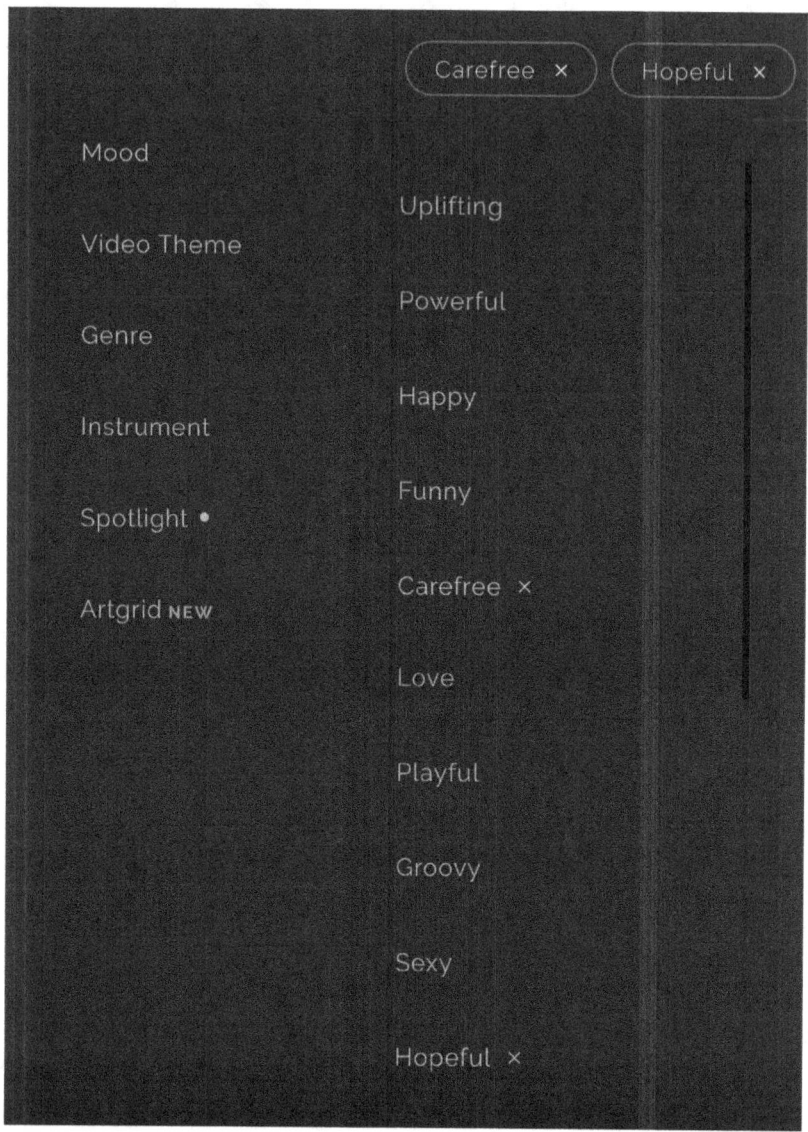

Artlist's Useful Search Filter

In addition to these, you can also filter it down further by searching for the exact duration that that music needs to be in your film

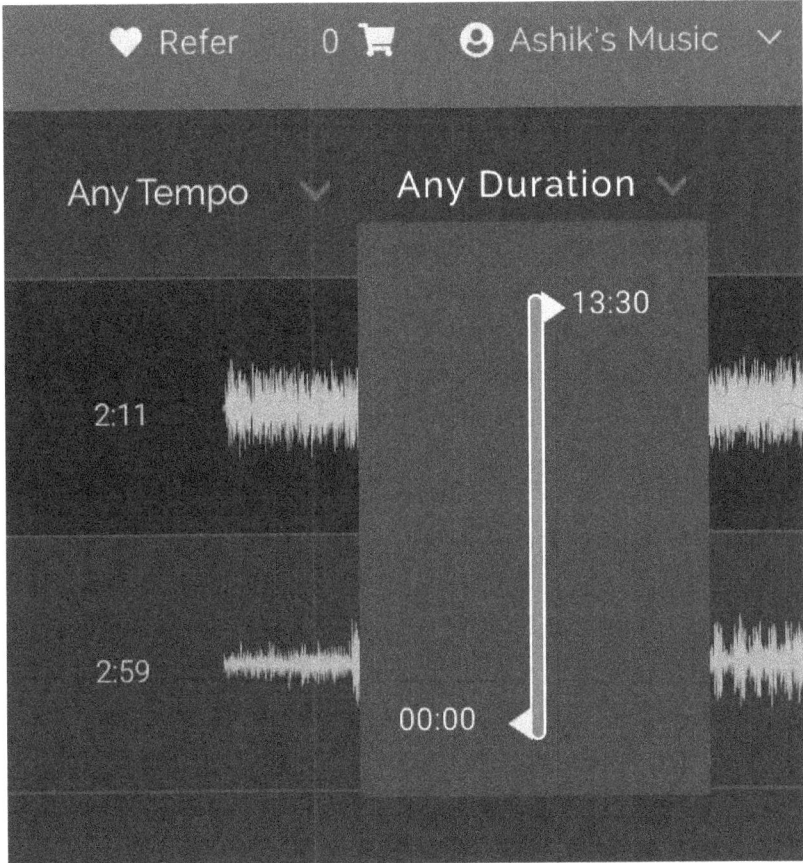

Artlist's Handy Time Filter

License

Whenever you download a song, you can also download the license file along with it. You will need these when you sell your film. Even after your subscription ends, you still own the license to the music. Important points you need to be careful on.

Price

Their licensing model is a one year subscription of $199 (₹14,500). It might seem a lot but I loved the collection of music, the easy search filters, and it was worth the time it saved me. Moreover we are still using Artlist to download songs for the videos that we are making and for ads and promos that our partner firm is making. Not a bad deal. Use referral link https://artlist.io/Ashik-491959 to get an additional 2 months.

Limitation

A limitation of Artlist is that you cannot download more than 40 tracks in a day. The first time I saw this it was irritating. I was short on time and I needed as much music as possible. But soon I realised I was not even using all the 40 tracks I downloaded. Hence I started curating using their folders and downloading only the songs that I was sure I needed.

Another limitation, not only of music from Artlist but in using any precomposed music, is that the music might not always begin and end on cue of your film. You might have to work this out with your sound engineer. We cut and pasted pieces of the music, shortened or extended it, used it from the middle or faded out in between, used louder sounds to distract the audience from the transition and so on. We even reedited some portions of the film to make it on cue with the music. These made the music feel as if it was composed for the film.

Alternatives

Alternatives to Artlist are websites like Premiumbeat, Epidemic Sound. I have not used any of these and hence cannot recommend. Please do your own research. Around 80-90% of all music you hear in *Munnariv* is from

Artlist. The remaining was created using a software called Filmstro.

Filmstro

Filmstro is the closest you can get to having music without a composer. The options we looked at before were all websites that had music made by composers, either given to us for free or at a fee. One of the major struggles you face with that is the music might not always be on cue with your film and at times you cannot edit the sequence and make it on cue. That is when we turned to Filmstro.

Filmstro[7] is a software with which you can dynamically change the music to make it go along with the film. They have a standalone software as well as add-ons that plug right into Adobe's Premiere Pro and Apple's Final Cut Pro. We used the standalone software as we were working on DaVinci Resolve.

License

All music you create during the time you have the subscription is licensed to you in perpetuity just like with Artlist. Though they do not have a ready to download license agreement, they promptly sent us one when we emailed them. It had a blanket approval for all their music.

Price

For feature films you would need the Pro Plus package. It costs $499 (₹35,500) for a year. Unlike Artlist, they do have a monthly subscription package, which costs $150 (₹10,500) for a project. We suggest taking

---

[7] For an introduction on what you can do with Filmstro, check the video titled 'Compose Music for Your Film' by the YouTube channel Film Riot, https://youtu.be/z9ebrSzDCbo

the monthly package. Be sure to have your edit almost locked, and as much music found from elsewhere, before taking this package. You will need time later to fine tune the music and maybe even reedit some parts of the film.

Limitation

Though it is fun to have such dynamically adjustable music, it does get tiring on the ears. It is after all music played in loops. Even though the volume, depth and momentum can all be changing, it is still the same melody that you are hearing over and over. In the hands of someone like Thomas Newman repeated melody is soothing and beautiful to hear. But not so much when it is done by a software.

Alternatives

I am not aware of any alternative softwares that can help you create dynamic music without a composer that is in sync with your film. But there are softwares coming up that uses Artificial Intelligence to create new music. One such website that I recently tried was aviva.ai. Though it intrigues me as an engineer, the music was far from satisfying. But give it a try.

How is the Final Music?

I asked almost everyone who saw *Munnariv* what they thought about the music. They all felt it was apt and nobody said anything particularly bad. One person even told me that they loved the music! One out of a hundred might not be much, but I have heard bad feedback on my choice of royalty free music in my previous short films. Considering that we seem to have done a fairly acceptable job. But let me not forever dissuade you from getting music composed for your film. Now that you know you can have music without a composer, let me tell you what we missed out on.

Limitations of Having Music Without A Composer

Besides an artistic collaboration, what we missed out on was storytelling through music. Because we are using precomposed music, we could not in any way vary it. In regular films for example, a character might have a certain melody attached to it. Think of Darth Vader from *Star Wars*[8]. With a composer we can vary the same piece of music to convey various emotions and stories[9].

Should You Get Music Without a Composer?

I wanted the music of *Munnariv* to tell such subtle stories. Which is why I had found someone to do the music for it. Maybe he quit on us because we were not paying him, or maybe he did not like the visuals, or maybe he had too much work at that time or maybe he was indeed sick as he claims. Whatever his reason might have been, accepting an advance, agreeing to do a project, and then not picking up calls when it was time to deliver, and quitting way past a mutually agreed deadline, is no way for a professional to work.

One of the good things about making films with no resources is that you find people who do stand with you because they trust you, your

---

8 To know more about the variety with which Darth Vader's music has been used throughout *Star Wars* check the video titled 'The Evolution of Darth Vader's Theme' by the channel Inside the Score youtu.be/LYGt8RwHVsE.

9 To learn how music was brilliantly used in Lord of the Rings to tell stories, watch this three part analysis video playlist youtube.com/playlist?list=PLaP_-iE-97d3JahtvcFKTXsZdpfWVkAkk.

vision or your project. And of course they would only be able to do that if they have some other means to cater to their day to day needs. All said, I am still grateful for what happened. Now you too know for certain that we can have reasonably acceptable music without a composer in any film that you may ever do. I now know how much more subtly I tell stories when I do work with a talented and professional composer.

Problems Are Only Challenges

I love challenges. Those that are just outside my comfort zone. What is the fun in doing something if not for the challenges! The steeper the mountain, the longer the climb lasts. The longer the climb, the hungrier I get. The hungrier I get, you better not stand in my way. For I fail to see anything but that which I am going for.

It is that laser sharp focus, the clarity of knowing the kind of music a particular scene needs, that got me through listening to thousands of tracks to find those perfectly fitting 50 pieces that the film needed. I am sure at least once in your life you too would have felt such laser sharp focus. Those moments that you now look back on, and wonder how in the world you did it. Problems are only challenges for you to become better. Bring that laser sharp focus to everything you do and make your film happen. If we can do it, you for sure can do it as well.

* * *

Foley and Ambience Sounds in Film's Sound Design

Much of storytelling through sound in films work at a level that is not very apparent. What we notice most are the dialogues and music. Foley and ambience sounds almost seems irrelevant. But the moment it is

94

not there you will find it distasteful, like a curry without salt. Foley and ambience sounds are what gives life, richness and texture to the soundscape.

Foley

Foley sound effects are all the sounds that we expect to hear associated with what we are seeing on screen. If a man is walking, then you have to hear footsteps. But is he walking on sand or concrete or tiles? Is it wet or dry? Is he wearing sandals or shoes or barefoot? All of these create a different sound[10]. It is attention to such minute details that adds to the texture and believability of what you are seeing on screen[11].

Ambience

Ambience sound effects are those sounds we expect to hear because of the place we are seeing on screen. A scene happening in a crowded cafe cannot sound empty. It needs to have lots of murmuring. A house in a village may have lots of birds chirping in the background, while a house in a city would have sounds of vehicles.

---

[10] To hear the difference foley adds to the experience watch the video titled 'The Magic of Making Sound' by the channel Great Big Story youtu.be/UO3N_PRIgXo.

[11] To know how you can record foley on your own, watch the video titled 'Foley Art | Episode 6: Indie Film Sound Guide' by the channel The Film Look after 1 minute 29 seconds youtu.be/zPHTMnQRjXg?t=89.

Recording Foley and Ambience Sounds for Munnariv

Our Sound Engineer handled every sound detail of our film. He wanted to record as much as was possible and use as little stock tracks as possible.

Foley in Munnariv

Our friend had a recording booth that was not being utilised. We cleaned up the place and used it to record clean foley. Every sound effect you hear in the film was recorded likewise.

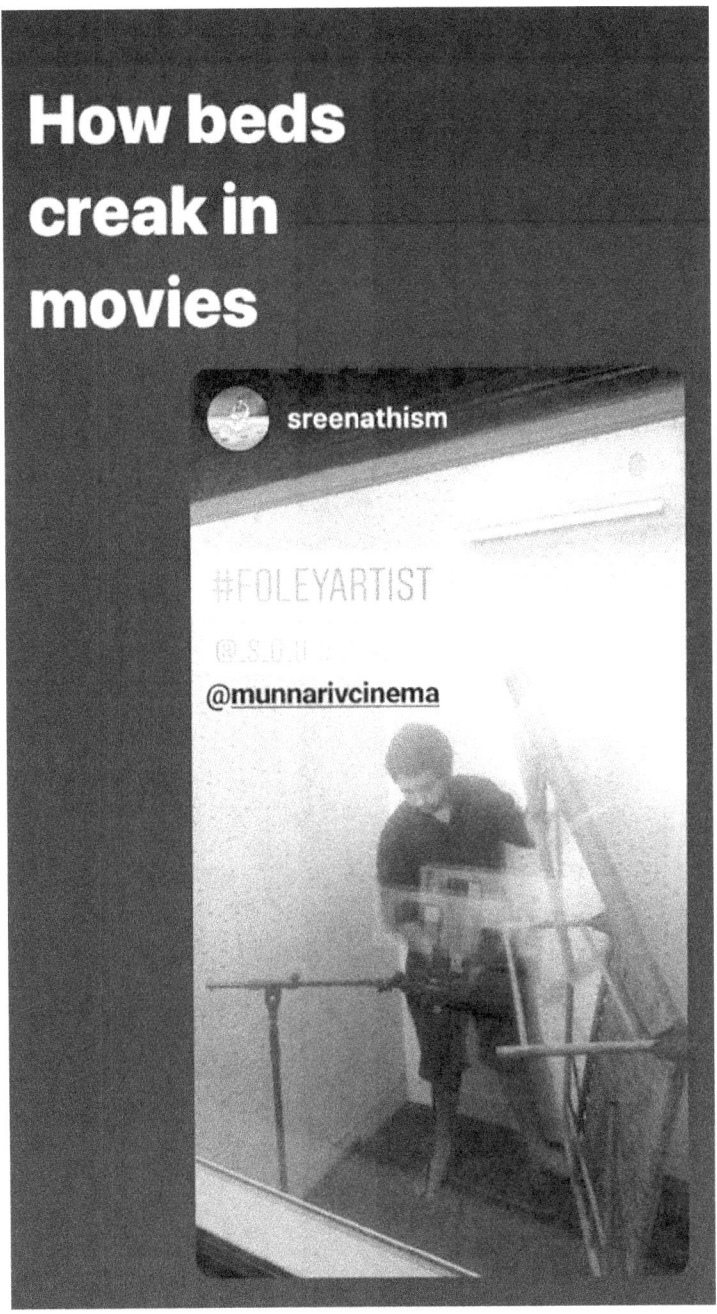

Recording Foley Sound Effects of Bed for Munnariv

Ambience in Munnariv

There are websites that provide free ambience tracks. But these all had people talking in English in the background, like kids playing while shouting in English, and so on. These are not the sounds of Kerala as we know it. Hence Sreenath went out with an old handy recorder we had, Zoom H4n, and recorded each of these individually.

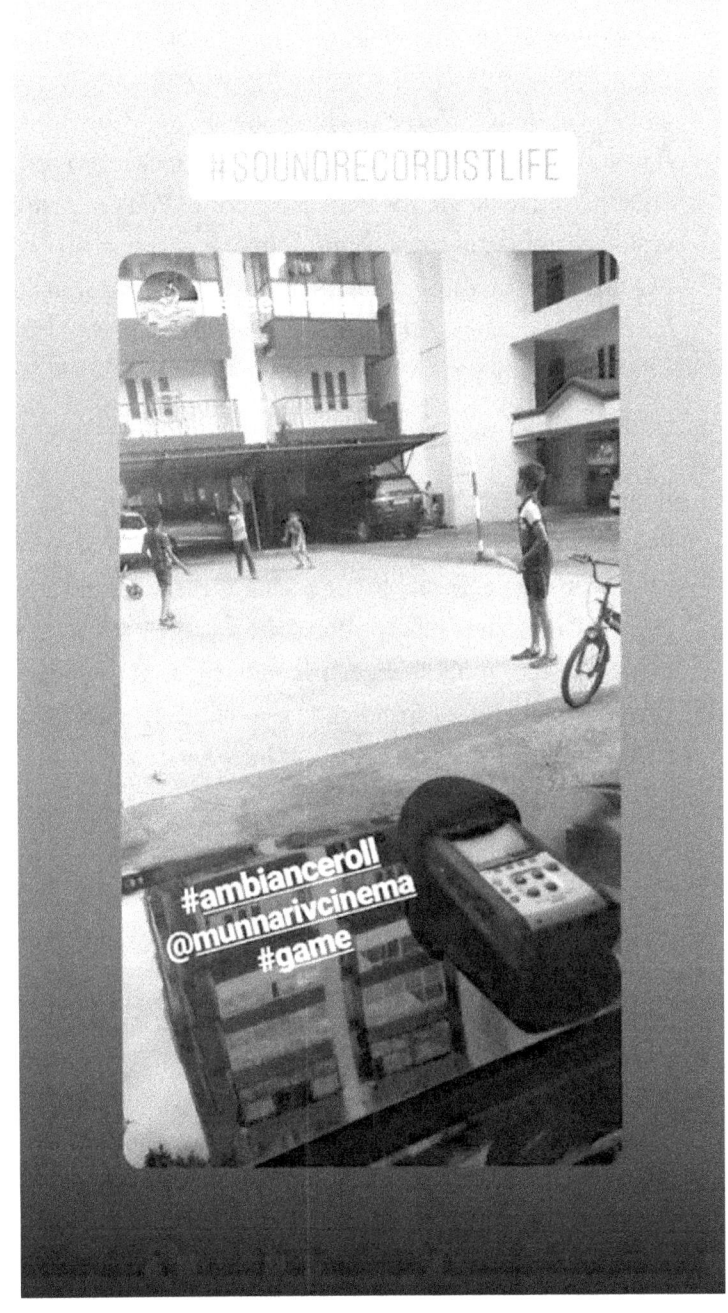

Recording Ambient Sounds of Children Playing for Munnariv

You need not wait for the postproduction stage to start recording ambience sounds. These can happen alongside the film's production. It is best to record foley once the picture is locked as each of the sound effects need to be in sync with the picture. You can also be collecting various samples of foley sounds. In one of our scenes we had a shot of a Shawarma being cut. Our Sound Engineer recorded various takes outside and later used the one that best matched with action on screen.

Soundly

Recording each sound is indeed a time consuming process. Some sounds, like footsteps can be easily found online. Soundly is a software through which you can get access to a lot of such free foley and ambience sound effects. Though it is subscription software, their free library has enough to get you started. To download Soundly, go to getsoundly.com. Besides Soundly, you can find such free to use sound effects on SoundCloud and a lot of other sites. Once all sounds have been found and aligned to the film, these then need to be mixed.

* * *

Sound Mixing and the Director's Job

Everything we do on set is nothing but collecting raw materials. It is in the editing table that a film actually comes together. Similarly it is in the Sound Mixing stage that all the sounds you've been collecting come together: the clean dialogues, the music you composed with or without a composer, the foley and ambience effects you recorded or found.

Mixing is the stage where all the sounds are brought together. Each element is mixed to make it seem appropriate for the scene and the film as a whole. Nonetheless I should admit that mixing is a topic that I am still learning. It was for this reason that I needed a Sound Engineer for *Munnariv*. I would listen to the stereo mix he created and if anything stood out, I would let him know.

What is Mixing

For *Munnariv* we identified all the basic elements—dialogues, music, foley and ambience—for each scene during preproduction itself. Our Sound Engineer religiously collected each of those sounds over time. Hence when it came to mixing the sounds it was a straightforward process. Generally the following is true for most scenes:

· Dialogue is the loudest
· Followed by the music
· Followed by the foley and ambience sounds

This is only a guideline[12]. If two people are standing by a drilling machine and is unable to hear the other, in spite of shouting at the top of their voices, then of course the mixing will reflect that. Among the countless videos online, the YouTube channel Cinema Sound by professional Sound Designer Mark Edward Lewis is one of the most legitimate ones. Worth checking out. Mark also has an online course on MZed for those looking to go in depth into the topic.

---

[12] For a beginner's guide on Sound Mixing check the video titled 'Mixing | Episode 8: Indie Film Sound Guide' by the channel The Film Look, youtu.be/7x5SnoftgUw. Not all of it might be accurate for a feature film.

What I Look for as a Director While Mixing

As a director my job is to hold the vision for what I want the audience to feel. I stand in for the audience and guide the crew to ensure that the audience is taken care of in every moment of the film. If you saw the video 'See With Your Ears: Spielberg And Sound Design' analysing a scene from Steven Spielberg's *Munich* I referenced earlier, you would know how beautifully sound designer Ben Burtt used sounds.

In *Munnariv* there is a scene in the beginning of the film where the lead character is in the toilet. There is a strange girl from nowhere sitting outside in his bedroom. He is tensed, scared and unsure what is going on. Instead of using a tense music, we chose to creatively use the ambient sound of the exhaust fan. We made it impressionistic of his mental state by making it louder and echoey than it would ever be, and menacingly slow. These are conscious choices we made in the mixing stage, working with the Sound Engineer. The audience will not consciously be aware of these, but will feel the danger or tension in it. There are no rules in art. It is then only by knowing why each scene exists that I, as a director, can know if something is right or wrong.

* * *

DaVinci Resolve, Your Best Friend in Postproduction

If you have been in the field, it is impossible to have not heard of the Australian company Blackmagic Design's software DaVinci Resolve. It is, and has been for years, the industry standard software for Color Correction.

What you might not know is that not only has Resolve gotten more powerful over the years, but it can now edit, dub, sound mix, do (minor)

VFX and output to almost all codecs. And in case you didn't know, it is free. The exact same software used by multimillion dollar blockbuster films like Wonder Woman, The Mummy and so on, can be used in your low budget film shot on a mobile phone in your bedroom.

Times Like None Other

Thirty years ago you had to spend a lot of money to make your film on film rolls. Then to edit it you had develop it, make copies, rent out an editing machine, physically cut the film (or make VHS cuts like Robert Rodrigues did in El Mariachi), stitch together film strips if you cut out an additional frame, develop negative, the positive, copies after copies. Just imagining it is giving me a headache. Do we live in times like none other or not!

Paid Version of DaVinci Resolve

They do have a studio version that lets multiple people work on the project simultaneously, exporting in resolutions over 4k, some additional feature like noise removal and so on. I do not believe you will find use of those right now. Noise removal was the only additional piece that we needed during the postproduction of *Munnariv*. For that we brought a plugin called Neat Video and did it.

Costs Comparison

- DaVinci Resolve: Free
- DaVinci Resolve Studio version: $300 (₹22,000), one time purchase
- Neat Video plugin: $70 (₹5,000) to $110 (₹8,000) depending on which software you want to plug into
- Adobe's standalone Premiere Pro: $20 (₹1,420) per month, that is

$230 (₹17,000) per year
- Whole Adobe suite: $600 (₹43,000) per year

Then there is of course the all evil cracked and pirated softwares. It is for most people where they start out. But now you know you have other options. Options that are not fiddley-medley. But solid industry grade softwares, for free. Get your free copy of DaVinci Resolve, go through the infinite tutorials on YouTube, and go make your film.

* * *

Create Subtitle for Your Film for Free

For years it was only films that went to festivals that needed a subtitle. With the ever increasing global penetration of YouTube and Over-The-Top (OTT) Platforms like Netflix and Amazon Prime Video, having subtitles for your film is soon becoming a necessity.

Why Subtitles

Right now the number of people watching films with subtitles is limited; mainly hardcore film buffs. But if you are looking to release your film on OTT platforms, then having subtitles is a must.

Subtitles open up your film to a wider audience, beyond the language your film is made in. This is of particular interest to us Indians as we have 22 working regional film industries. No one speaks all the 22 languages. Not even 3 of these. Okay some might. My point is, on average an educated Indian knows English alongside their mother tongue. By having English subtitles even if you are reaching only one additional person, that counts! Also, once your film has English subtitles, now it can be easily be converted into any of the 22 regional languages or any of the world languages.

What You Need to Make Subtitles

If you feel it is worth creating subtitles for your film, what you need to go ahead are the following two things:

- A software to position the subtitles appropriately
- Knowledge of both languages to translate effectively

Let us look at two free softwares that can help you with timing the text.

Subtitle Edit

Subtitle Edit is a freeware that you can use to create subtitles for videos of any length, be it a 10 minute video, a 3 hour feature film. A feature film you would of course not have such a long file. It would be cut into many reels as we discussed earlier. It is a fairly easy to use and a self-evident software. There are a lot of tutorials online to guide you through the whole process. You can export the subtitle as an SRT file—a widely supported format.

YouTube

YouTube has a web application that lets you create subtitles. The advantage of using this over Subtitle Edit is that it automatically identifies all the spots where human voice is present and places a text accordingly. It makes your work easier. It even automatically transcribes the text for you. But this is far from being reliable as of now. Especially so if the language is not English. I would not suggest using YouTube's subtitle creator if you are making a feature film. It can come in handy in placing texts. But beyond that it is very limited. For example, when working in reels, it does not let you combine the subtitle files.

Subtitle Creator in Editing Softwares

Adobe Premiere Pro, DaVinci Resolve and all have their own inbuilt subtitle creators. I have only used this once and never liked it. My mind kept wandering to the edits instead of concentrating on the translation. I prefer to use a dedicated software meant for making subtitles.

Translation Knowledge

This can be a challenge for some, and a breeze for others. Not everyone is skilled in translating the nuances of one language to another.

Translating a book requires proficiency in both the languages. In addition to that, one who is creating subtitles need to know the colloquial usages in both the languages, the meaning of certain usages per territory and so on. These are more advanced topics. Professional subtitle creators are experts in various languages and hence expensive to hire. But if you already wrote the dialogues for your film, and if you are reading this, then translating your dialogues to good English can be easily done.

Future Proofing Your Film

More and more people are now getting used to watching videos in languages that they don't understand. Right now it might be because they have a strong need to learn something. Slowly, but surely, we will get accustomed to reading subtitles.

It is only natural that over the course of years, a significant portion of the population would go beyond informative videos. It could be possible that they start enjoying films too with subtitles. Create subtitles for your film, and reach a wider audience today and tomorrow.

* * *

Transcoding Your Film Using HandBrake

Transcoding is the process of transferring files in one format to another, say from MP4 to AVI. In the postproduction phase of making your film, you would regularly need to transcode your film. HandBrake is one option to compress the film.

For example, when you are finished with a reel, you will have to send it out to various people. The Grading and VFX teams would need the humungous high quality files, which runs into the GB and TB ranges. If you want to send a copy to the producer or a friend for feedback, you cannot of course upload such huge files. And the sound team would need the files to be under 100 MB.

Why Not Transcode in The Editing Software?

You may use the project in your editing software itself to transcode the film. But the system would have to go through countless video files spread across your hard disk, or even multiple hard disks, to provide you with the final output; depending on the complexity of the edit. If something goes wrong, then you would have to do the whole thing again. Also repeatedly opening the master project file is taking on unnecessary risks. You might accidentally shift a cut by two seconds and not even realise it.

Only use your editing software to export a high quality version of the reel. Preferably export in ProRes format. Then use a dedicated software like HandBrake to transcode it into a compressed codec and send to whoever you want to.

HandBrake for Transcoding

HandBrake is again a freeware. I use it regularly to transcode the huge ProRes or CineForm files into manageable MP4 files. It is available for Mac and PC. To download, go to handbrake.fr/downloads.

Limitations of HandBrake

HandBrake currently supports exporting only into MP4 and MKV formats. So far I have never come across a situation where a compressed format beyond these two were asked for. Amazon Prime and other OTT platforms would require the high quality ProRes versions anyway. Another limitation is that it is not the most easy to use software for a first timer[13].

* * *

What is DCP and What It Costs

Filmmakers moving to features need to be aware of Digital Cinema Package or DCP. It is a digital standard followed across the globe

---

[13] To reduce your video's file size by almost one tenth while retaining the quality at the same time check the video titled 'How To Upload Videos To YouTube FAST! Best Handbrake Settings For YouTube' by channel Muaaz, youtu.be/yOIv31SYkkw.

to enable seamless projection in any theatre, of any film produced anywhere in the world. An easy way to think of it is like the frames you saw in the olden day films.

The celluloid films used to have a lot of frames printed on it and a sound track to the side. The projector played each frame and the corresponding sound using the perforations as a guide. Unlike the single file torrent downloads you might be used to, the whole film is exported as individual images and separate sound tracks of very high quality. It is the perforations that guided the old projectors when to play what. In digital, the DCP holds all the images and sounds and guides the projector when to play what.

How To Create DCP?

It is something you can do on your own[14], but I would advice against it. Outsource it to professionals. I think it costs something between $130 (₹10,000) to $400 (₹30,000) (need to check in your area). You might be able to beg your way into playing a BluRay, but all major festivals need you send them DCPs. If you plan to release in movie theatres, DCP is a must. Anyway you do not want playback issue when 100 people are in their seats waiting to see your film. I want our film to play like butter. And if there is some hiccup, I want to call the expert who made the DCP and get the problem solved quickly.

A DCP file easily goes over 2, 4 TB. I have only seen DCPs in professional quality external hard drives, the ones with external power. Never in a portable pocket disk, except for backups. All good quality ones will cost at least $270 (₹20,000). And to be on the safer side, you need 2 of the same hard drives to make two copies. In case you made only one DCP,

---

14 To create DCP on your own, https://noamkroll.com/how-to-make-any-dcp-for-25-with-davinci-resolve-15-kakadu-cinematiq/

and you lost it somehow, then you will have to spend money to recreate the DCP and on hard drives. Up to you.

If Only Releasing Online

Then you do not have to worry about DCP. ProRes files are fairly standard across all online streaming platforms. It is easy to create if you have a Mac, or the latest version of Adobe Premiere Pro. Just be aware that there is such a thing as DCP and what it is going to cost you.

* * *

6

Marketing and Selling

We live in a time like none other. What once took immense patience, energy and resources to do, can now be done on a device the size of your palm. At the same time, getting your film in front of an audience has become tough. This has made marketing an integral part of filmmaking.

> *"I think there are more films being made, but there are probably less outlets for them and distributors."—Richard Linklater*

Trust

Have you ever seen a film's poster that had actors whom you had no idea about, made by a director you have never heard of, and still went to a theatre to see it? I need at least some kind of assurance that it will be worth my time. What stars have built, in a sense, is that trust factor. Anyone who goes for a Rajinikanth film knows what he/she is going to get. Over the years we have gotten so used to seeing Mohanlal and Aamir Khan that it is like going to see an old friend. When a Rajkumar Hirani or Christopher Nolan or Marvel film is out, we know for sure it is going to be engaging. They have earned our trust.

Awareness

Knowing that something exists, that is awareness, is also a part to the puzzle. All franchises, stars and star directors have a huge fan following. As soon as a major star's next film is announced, newspapers follow it up, people tweet about it. In addition to that they also put up huge billboards and run ads in newspapers TV, radio and other social media platforms. When you have neither the audience's trust nor the money, how are you going to make people aware that your film exists? Why should someone talk about your film? Why should they even care?

Being Remarkable

> *"The thing that's going to decide what gets talked about, what gets done, what gets changed, what gets purchased, what gets built, is is it remarkable?"—Seth Godin*[15]

Remarkable not only means "nice", but it also means "worth making a remark about". Aamir Khan's 5 minutes body transformation video for *Dangal* had over 39 million views. *Avatar* was released in the biggest financial depression we have seen and still people flocked to watch it because of its magical visual effects. It is awe inspiring even after a decade. What is that compelling thing about your film that people cannot help but tell their friends about it?

---

[15] For more information on being remarkable, watch the TED Talk titled 'How to get your ideas to spread | Seth Godin' youtu.be/xBIVlM435Zg.

How Munnariv is Remarkable

Munnariv is the first ever Malayalam Sci-Fi feature film to be shot entirely on an iPhone SE. It was the reason why we were able to get a national newspaper like *The Hindu* to feature a writeup about it even while it was in production[16]. For anyone who has seen the film, they find it so well shot that they cannot believe we made it on a mobile, like the one they have in their pockets. Add to that a story so unique and surprising. People want to tell their friends about it. Even before the release I had friends asking if they could have a private link to watch *Munnariv*.

Think again about that question. How is your film remarkable? What is that one thing that people want to talk about? When you have no stars or money to market, having something organically worth talking about is the only way of spreading word about your film. Do it well and get marketing for free. *Munnariv's* journey has only begun and only time will tell how far it will go. But I hope I have been able to get across to you the importance of marketing. But marketing is not selling. It only builds awareness. Selling is a different game and we'll talk about it tomorrow.

* * *

Why People Pay to Watch Films

Imagine you bought a new mobile phone. You turned it on. It displays some random images and then turned off. You turn it on again, the same thing happens. You take it back to the shop you bought it from

---

[16] Read the article about *Munnariv* that came on *The Hindu* https://www.thehindu.com/todays-paper/tp-features/tp-metroplus/a-phone-story/article26616216.ece

and ask for a replacement. But the shopkeeper tells you that "you don't understand, that it is a piece of art. The edge of the phone is perfectly curved like no other phone has ever been able to. You are paying to watch the most beautiful photos ever taken by man." This is what he intended when he made the phone and he is not going to repay you. You are either going to take him to court or maybe crack his head. When you pay for something, you expect it to deliver a certain value in return.

What People are Paying For

Filmmaking, to me, is both an art and a business. If you are in for the art, film as a form of self indulgent self expression, then by all means do that. But do not expect the world to pay to watch and applaud your masterpiece. If you want people to pay for something you create, you need to deliver them something of value in return.

> "A novel or short story can have, in a sense, no story or dramatic progression, no conflict or crisis. Maybe some forms of experimental and personal cinema have little need for dramatic tension, but a narrative fiction film is (more often than not) something else. Dramatic tension generally requires an element of conflict."—Alexander Mackendrick

People pay to watch films at the cinema halls because they want to see drama, tension, conflict. Even the best of romance and comedy works only when there is conflict; the girl's father opposes the boy, or if it is a comedy it could be the girl's dog, and story goes around how the boy resolves these conflicts.

Asking to Pay to Watch

Your film's trailer, its posters, are all giving the audience a certain promise that the film will deliver a certain something if you pay to watch it. If it is comic in nature, people expect to laugh. If tragic in nature, people expect to cry. If it has a lot of set pieces, people expect a blockbuster and so on.

> *"Drama is life with the dull bits cut out." — Alfred Hitchcock*

Even as you read through this book, you are expecting to learn something out of it. My promise could be the title, the summary you might have seen, the first few pages, the way it is written and structured and so on. Had I been beating around the bush and not getting to the topic you would have left already.

By all this I do not mean to demean personal artistic cinema. My films are all personal to me. But at the same time I am aware that I am in a business transaction and that I need to deliver. I try to ride a line in the middle. If the film you want to make is an artistic self expressive piece then please do that. Film festivals and cinema halls that screen art house films might be your way to go. They too make a lot of money, though perhaps less glamorous. Forgive my ignorance in the regard.

Your Film's Value

Films with an artistic merit that is meant to be consumed need to deliver. Being artists, filmmakers are not usually concerned about its business aspects. We are probably not used to selling either. But while making a low budget film that you are planning to distribute yourself, it is important you know that you are asking someone to pay to watch it. Even if it is an artistic expression, you are in a business transaction, perhaps for a different audience. They are bearing the expenses of flying down to a film festival because they are looking for something. It is your job, as the creator, to be aware of the value your film is offering, to whoever the audience you believe it is for. This will guide you in the steps ahead, of selling your film, be it through cinema halls, film festivals or other means.

* * *

Difference between Marketing and Sales of Films

Marketing is not sales. It is all the activities that result in building awareness and desire for a product. While selling is the actual act of giving someone something they need, in return for a payment. It is a distinction that you need to understand. Let me explain.

Marketing and Sales of Films

For commercially released movies, the posters, billboards, and Ads (in newspapers, radio, TV, social media) and critical reviews all help increase awareness of the film. These let us know that a certain film is releasing on a certain date. It usually lasts till the film leaves the theatres. For art house films, marketing is based off of all the critical acclaim it received; the festivals it had been to, the awards and critical reviews it received and so on. Building on top of that you could get a theatrical release and repeat the marketing process of a commercial movie.

But marketing does not bring you back the money. That is what selling is. Sales is what happens when a person pays to watch the film. It can be in a theatre, on a streaming service, on DVD, on TV and so on. If the

116

film is good, this can happen forever.

Good Marketing

Just for a moment, think of bread. Did you think of it in slices? But when sliced bread was invented, no one wanted it. 15 years later 'Wonder' figured out how to market it. That changed bread's identity forever and we have the sliced bread that we so regularly use. Without good marketing, that is raised awareness and desire for something, any good product is bound to fail.

Sales Forever

Is there a film that you've watched over and over? You might sit and watch it again if it was airing tomorrow on your TV. A good film, which is marketed well, can be making sales for as long as it exists. Once your film has hit the theatres, do not think its journey is over. There are so many films that flopped at the box office, but turned into cult classics over the years. If your film is good, it could be making money even 50 years later.

Summing up, marketing is the building up of awareness and desire for your film; by winning awards at festivals, running ads, word of mouth, and so on. While sales is that which happens every time you earn money from the film. If you are going to distribute your film, it is important that you understand the difference between marketing and selling. Moreover, I believe in the eyes of a seasoned producer, these experiences and knowledge will increase your value as a filmmaker.

* * *

Selling Your Film on Amazon Prime

Now that you see marketing and sales of films differently, and understand that sales happen forever, let us look at one of the options of selling your film today, on Amazon Prime. As of writing this, YouTube, Hotstar, Prime and Netflix are the streaming platforms In India with the user base. Of these, Prime is the most accessible because of Amazon Prime Video Direct.

Note: As of writing this book Munnariv has not be put on Amazon Prime Video. Following are from our research and not from experience.

What is Amazon Prime Video Direct

It is a platform through which you can sell your film on Amazon. It runs with the tagline, "Helping studios, distributors, and independent filmmakers reach audiences worldwide". There are two options of selling through Prime Direct:

- Rent/Buy
- Included With Prime

First of all, please know that there is no upfront payment. You market your film, you bring customers to the Prime page, they watch, you earn a small amount. Prime acts as only a marketplace. There are thousands of other films there and you need good marketing to stand out.

With Rent/Buy you are not selling your film on Prime. But people can rent or buy it on Amazon. You get 50% of what each customer pays. If you are looking for that, Vimeo On Demand might be a better option as you get 90% of a sale. With 'Included With Prime' option, your film is accessible to anyone on Prime. How you get payed is on the hours watched.

Dependence of Earnings on Viewership

The rates of payment have drastically been cut down over the year we have been following Prime Direct. Also your payout is highly dependent on a ranking system that keeps track of your content's performance every year. As stated by Amazon, Customer Engagement Ranking is calculated based on the following:

- Unique members who view your title
- Time each customer spends engaging with your content
- Notable talent, relevant genres, an IMDb presence and rating, and box office performance
- Compelling and high-quality poster art, accurate and representative copy and metadata, localised subtitles and key art

Possible Earnings in Selling Your Film on Prime

For one person watching your film for an hour, it can be as low as 71 paise and the highest being around $0.12 (₹ 8.5). Let us assume your film is an hour and half long and every month you make 1000 people watch your film on Prime. Then you might get around $170 (₹ 13,000) that year. If you make 15,000 people watch every month, then you get between 12 to 22 lakhs that year.

How do you get 1000 or 15,000 people to watch? You put money into marketing every month. Let us assume that you put Facebook and Instagram Ads. You need 1000 people to watch every month. Not everyone you bring to you film's page on Prime is going to watch it. Let us say 10 % of all those who come will watch your film. That means you have to bring 10,000 people to you page each month.

To bring 10,000 people to your page, you need to reach 2,50,000, assuming a modest click rate of 4% on your Ads. To reach 2,50,000 unique people every month you will have to spend around $40 (₹3,000) (only an approximation, roughly calculated by our recent Ads spend). So for a film with no stars but good reviews, (based on a lot of assumptions) to get:

- the minimum earning of $170 (₹13,000) a year, i.e a low Customer Engagement Ranking, you might have to spend $540 (₹40,000) in marketing
- the maximum earning of $30,000 (₹22,00,000) a year, i.e a high Customer Engagement Ranking, you might have to spend $8,000 (₹6,00,000)

Going big looks to be the only option, if you have $8,000 (₹6,00,000) to spend on Ads.

How To Sell Your Film on Prime

Putting you film on Prime is a straight forward process that requires some work. Linking to a video with detailed explanation on how to go about it[17].

Why Munnariv is Not on Prime

One of our concerns is that with the increasing number of content, ranking high every year might not be practically possible, without strong marketing or positive word of mouth. But these are all assumptions that we can only know by doing it.

Also once your film is on Prime, or any other online platform for that matter, your film can no longer be sent to any of the major film

---

[17] How to sell your film on Amazon Prime youtu.be/KfcEM0ED_ws.

festivals. These were some of the reasons why sent the film to festivals first. The right path for your film depends on what you are looking for. We are merely presenting our study in hopes that you can verify them for yourselves and make better decisions.

Note: I could not find the current rate Amazon pays for India. You can read the current international rate card[18] and agreement details[19] after signing up for an account on Amazon Video Central.

Dollar Account

If you do decide to go the Amazon Prime Direct route, you need one additional thing. When you try to set up your account they will ask you for your bank details. When you say you reside in India, it will give you an error. All it will say is that Amazon Prime Direct does not support electronic payments to any Indian banks. I was left baffled and not sure what to do. A month long attempt to get a solution from their customer service was absolutely worthless.

But it was when I went to Goa with *Munnariv*, that I found the answer, a Dollar Account. It is an account facility that most banks have. It lets you accepts payments in US Dollars instead of Indian Rupees, even when you are in India. You can easily have the amount converted and deposited to any account of your choosing. Making purchases with that account is restricted as far as I know.

All you need to do is go to your bank and ask to start a Dollar Account or technically, a Resident Foreign Currency (Domestic) account and follow the procedure like opening any other account. We are in the process of setting one up.

---

[18] Amazon Prime's international rate card videocentral.amazon.com/home/royalty-rates

[19] Amazon Video Central agreement details videocentral.amazon.com/home/agreement

* * *

What VOD Costs

Video-On-Demand (VOD) platforms are aplenty today and will keep increasing in numbers for some years to come. Among them which to choose, how to go about it, what it costs, are questions I needed answers to and probably you too. Let's look at aggregators.

What is an Aggregator?

From what I understand, aggregators are companies that collect, or aggregate, various films and then pitch it as a suite of films to VOD platforms. For VOD platforms they act as a single point of access to a collection of films that meet their technical requirements. For filmmakers they act as a pathway to VOD platforms. One such aggregator that we have been looking into is Quiver.

How We Used Quiver

More than using Quiver to distribute our film, what we used it for is to help figure out how much it would cost to do so and what all the elements are. The following is from our study. These are not to be taken as endorsements or as our experience.

The following breaks down, to the minutest detail, what it would cost us to sell *Munnariv* on YouTube (through Google Play) and on iTunes, if we went through Quiver. It also details what each item would cost.

Order Breakdown

Description	Qty	Price	
Base Package Includes - 1 Title, 1 Retailer, and 1 Language	1	$1,395.00	
REQUIRED	10		
Open Retailers	2	$225.00	
Google Play	1		$225.00
iTunes (Included in Base Package)	1		$0.00
Territory	1	$0.00	
Videos	3	$0.00	
Closed Captions and Subtitles	1	$500.00	
English Subtitles - Feature	1		$500.00
Artwork	2	$25.00	
Main Poster Art (Included in Base Package)	1		$0.00
India CBFC Certificate	1		$25.00
Ratings	1	$0.00	
India Rating (Included in Base Package)	1		$0.00

Total: $2145.00

Estimated Expenses of Quiver to Put Munnariv on YouTube and iTunes

You need the Censor Board certificate if you want to distribute in India through Quiver. Quiver does not do this for you. You will have to go the office yourself and get this done. This will add an additional $700 (₹50,000) (approximate figure) to your budget, for the screening, DCP costs and so on.

There are such similar requirements for different territories. For example, if you want your film to be accessible to people in Germany/France, then the film must have German/French subtitles. If you want your film in the United States, then you need to pay for Closed Captions, and so on. Go to distribute.quiverdigital.com. Make an account and test these for the needs of your particular film. It is free.

Using Quiver For Distribution

If you do go the Quiver route, then you would have to pay the $2,000 (₹ 1.5 lakhs) upfront. Plus the censor certificate expense of $700 (₹50,000), if you do not have one already. Having not gone through this route yet, we are not sure of all the implications of the 2 year term. Their renewal fee of ₹5500 for two years is almost negligible if the film makes any money at all. And unlike other aggregators, you get to keep all the royalties the film earns during the 2 years.

Quiver also gives you access to other VOD platforms, such as Netflix, for an additional application fee of $140 (₹10,500) for each. Paying this fee does not guarantee that your film will be put up on Netflix. It is merely a pitching fee and your film may or may not be approved. Quiver does not seem to support Amazon Prime Video in India right now. It used to, while we were exploring 2 years ago. VOD is the thing right now. Even if you get your films up on these platforms, the onus of getting people aware of it, of marketing and selling your film, is still on you. It comes with its own share of expenses and problems. We hope this article shines light on Quiver and how you can use it.

* * *

Beyond Releasing Online

Over-the-top (OTT) media service is all the internet streaming services, like Prime, Netflix, YouTube and so on. This is a platform did not exist 10 years ago and has been rising since. Though it could be where your low budget films might finally reside, let me show your other options and why OTT should only be the last option.

Theatrical Release

> *"The theatrical marketplace is a challenge. What do you have to do to get someone to purchase a movie ticket to your movie? You have to do something that they've never seen before; you've got to enthrall them in a new way."*—Richard Linklater

If you had managed to get a named actor in your film then you might have the possibility of getting a theatrical release. I would highly suggest you watch a TED Talk by Manish Mundra of Drishyam Films[20]. Drishyam Films produced acclaimed films like *Masaan*, *Waiting* and so on. In the talk he shares the following overall economics of his films:

- Production: $300,000 (₹2 crores)
- Music + miscellaneous: $70,000 (₹0.5 crores)
- Print promotion and Ads: $330,000 (₹2.5 crores)
- Govt. Subsidies: − $135,000 (₹1 crores)

Net cost of exhibited film: $540,000 (₹4 crores)

- Theatrical collection: $200,000 to $300,000 (₹1.5 to ₹2 crores)
- Digital/Satellite: $300,000 to $400,000 (₹2 to ₹3 crores)
- Misc. exploitation: $300,000 to $540,000 (₹2 to ₹4 crores)
- International sales: $400,000 to $810,000 (₹3 to ₹6 crores)

Net revenue: $540,000 to $810,000 (₹4 to ₹6 crores) (after fees and deductions)

What surprised me—and what I want you to take note of as well—were two things:

---

[20] Business of Indie Film Making | Manish Mundra | TEDxMICA youtu.be/u4Myy1yJWOo

- The amount spent on marketing the film. It is just as much as or if not more that the cost of producing the film.
- The collection beyond theatrical. It is more than five times the box office collection.

Of course it is the marketing for the theatrical release and the later theatrical success that leads to satellite sales and others. But unless you are Martin Scorsese with an Oscar nominated film like *The Irishman*, releasing your film on an OTT platform alone and waiting for the money to roll in, might not be the best option.

Film Festivals

Premiering *Munnariv* in a world reputed film festival; that is where we planned to kickstart *Munnariv*'s journey. The world's top 5 festivals, and other few ones, have associated with them markets that have impact. There will be other festival programmers, international distributors, OTT platforms, all looking for new reputed content. There are an infinite number of blogs that talks about which festivals to apply, how to an so on. What I will share with you are the festivals you need to look out for.

The Big 5

The biggest 5 festivals are the following:

- Cannes or Festival de Cannes - Of course the most famous. Open till February
- Berlinale or Berlin International Film Festival - Closes November
- Venice International Film Festival - Opens February
- Sundance Film Festival - Everyone applies here. Opens around June.
- Toronto International Film Festival - The largest fest

These festivals receive thousands of film submissions each year.

Other Notable Festivals

Getting your film into the big 5 might be a little difficult without resources. Following are some other festivals worth looking at:

- Locarno Film Festival - Opens February.
- Busan International Film Festival - October
- International Film Festival Rotterdam - Opens July.
- Telluride Film Festival - Happens in April.
- Hong Kong International Film Festival - Opens in September.
- Raindance Film Festival - Opens September.
- International Film Festival of India - India's biggest. Happens in November.
- Other reputed state wise international film festivals.

Though these might not have the market impact that the big 5 has, they are still festivals that people visit. Any place where you can be seen along with your film, and the audience loves it, it is a joy to be there. You never know when and where serendipity can happen. You might meet the connection you were looking for and they might find the film they were looking for.

Film Freeway

filmfreeway.com is a website that makes application to film festivals a piece of cake. You can fill out the application once, upload the film to Film Freeway and then onwards apply to any festival by just paying their fees. For the major festivals we talked about previously you are still going to have to go through their site and apply. Film Freeway not only has festivals for feature films, but for shorts, web series, screenplays, and so on. Some festivals even have zero application fees. There was a similar site called Withoutabox that Amazon owned. But it is now shut down.

Film Bazaar

What is Film Bazaar? Who is it for? Why is the entry fee $200 (₹15,000) while International Film Festival of India (IFFI) is just $14 (₹1,000)? These were the questions that were in my mind while I was thinking of going there for the first in 2019.

For people who do not know what Film Bazaar is, in short it is as the name says, a market to buy and sell film. The number of sellers is far more than buyers in the current economic scenario of India. It is the biggest film market we have in India. Is it worth paying $200 (₹15k)? Yes. The free Marriott buffet is alone worth $80 (₹6k). You get free drinks every night, along with free tea, coffee, biscuits all the time. You get a leather goody bag. Plus knowledge series sessions that are more focused than the ones at IFFI.

Then you get to meet people, which is the part where your soft skills come into play. I am still developing the skills to introduce myself to people and talk to them about my project. I am a good listener though. What you give up are the good films you get to watch at IFFI for the first four or five days. For makers, the best time to go there is when you have a project there, be it in Script Lab, Viewing Room, Industry Screening, Work in Progress, Coproduction Market and so on. For buyers it's very obvious when to go. Check filmbazaarindia.com for more information. It happens alongside IFFI, during November end.

Licensing

Beyond all that we discussed so far—theatrical, digital, festivals, international sales—there are even more ways to make money off a film. What we need to understand is that a film is an Intellectual Property (IP). You own the IP for at least 80 years. Following are some fo the ways you can exploit it.

Books

Did you see the novel version of *Bahubali?* I think there was a comic version or a children's version as well. I am not sure. Let us not look at Bahubali being released as a video game, but if you wrote the script of your film, can you turn it into a story?

India's biggest publishers might not come and pay you an advance to do that, or they might (who knows), but what you can do is self publish it. Check out Amazon Kindle Direct Publishing[21]. You can publish your book as an eBook for no upfront cost. If you want to have it print, there are countless sites that print-on-demand and sell on Amazon/Flipkart. You do not have to print hundreds of copies and store in your house. They print only when they receive an order. You do not have to worry about anything. You can either hire people to do all this for you. If you do not have the money, then spend time learning and then do it yourself.

Remakes

The strength of India is its diversity. If your film was proven successful in one regional language then it might be easier to convince someone to remake it in another language. Did you know there are over 22 working

---

[21] Amazon Kindle Direct Publishing https://kdp.amazon.com

regional film industries in India? If remaking is too expensive you can maybe have it dubbed. If that is too expensive, maybe subtitled. But that would reduce the reach considerably to English speaking people and defeat the purpose of accessing regional industries.

Music Rights

This is a fairly standard practice. If you had hired the composer, you can sell the music.

In-flight Entertainment

If you have traveled on airlines you would have seen films on it. One company does it in India which is Shemaroo Entertainment's subsidiary, Contentino Media[22]. If your film is in the genre of romance or comedy, it does not have guns and violence, and no flight bombings, you might have a good chance. If the film is good you can earn anything from $7,000 to $40,000 (₹ 5,00,000 to ₹30,00,000) in a year. You can get that year after year if your film is good and if people are asking for it. There are people even today buying the rights of old MGR and NTR films. I saw an old film at a film festival that was rereleased with an updated 5.1 soundtrack.

What I want you to realise is the value of the IP that you have created. You will earn your money back. But do not expect to make a film today and earn the money tomorrow. It will take time, but you definitely can earn it back.

* * *

---

[22] In-flight entertainment company https://www.shemarooent.com/inflight/

Having Fun Making Films

The journey of making a film is like taking the 25 years journey of a baby—from infancy to adulthood—and rapidly rushing through it in a year or two. Filmmaking is arduous. During those nerve-racking times 'fun' might not be the feeling you always have.

When It is Not Fun Making Films

What starts as an idea between the ears of one person, is transformed into something tangible by the hands and minds of hundreds, to finally become an idea again between the ears of millions. That is filmmaking. Days on set making a film are laborious. But if you have chosen your team carefully in preproduction, the days on set are also the most fun times you'll always fondly remember.

For low budget films, postproduction, marketing and selling your film can be lonely times. Nothing might seem to be working out as you had hoped for. You can find yourself in your worst nightmares. During those times again remind yourself that you are only making a film and to have fun. Let your mind wander. Let it come up with random solutions; without worrying about it being right or wrong. Let it flow. Talk to a friend and laugh at the silliness. Watch a film. Read a book. Do whatever you may have to do.

The Carefree Mind

It is during those fun moments, when your mind and body is relaxed, that you get to be that curious and creative child again. It is only in that carefree state that you get to experiment fearlessly. Out of those fun tinkering might come something more beautiful than you could have ever imagined.

Slowly but surely, as you keep walking towards your destination, changing the route as often as required to get there, you will seeing things working out. As you keep moving forward again the light at the end starts becoming brighter and brighter. Whatever the outcome might be, it never lasts for more than a day or two. But it is the journey towards it that is always going to be the longest. So enjoy the problems. Take it as a challenge. Come up with creative solutions and have fun making your film!

* * *

7

Beyond Filmmaking

Throughout this book we talked about filmmaking. I have shared with you everything I learned in my journey so far. I hope it gives you an idea of the possibilities of the time we live in. Before we part ways, I wanted to bring to your attention to some things that are beyond our topic of filmmaking, but I feel are necessary.With the principles of making a low budget film you can now turn any story into a film without waiting for big stars or lots of money. When that is the case, our judgement as a filmmaker becomes a lot more important.

Judgement

When it is all said and done, and your film is ready, what if no one likes it? What if no one resonates with your creation? It satisfies only your need for wanting to create something and adds no value or meaning to someone else; which in itself can be a great achievement. But not if you want to make a living as a filmmaker. We buy things to satisfy our needs. When anyone can turn any story into a film, how do we decide which story is worth telling? Not only does making a film need a lot more time and resources than writing a story, there is a lot more at stake. And hence as filmmakers we need to cultivate the skill of critically judging our own story.

> *"Judgment is knowing the long-term consequences of your actions."—Naval Ravikant*[23]

How to Cultivate Judgement as a Filmmaker

Rewatch films you like and figure out what you liked about it. But more importantly, rewatch films you do not like and figure out why you did not like it. It is from the films I detest that I have learned the most from. Put it into words exactly why you did not like. Think on questions such as, was it the story that was not engaging, or was it how it was miscast? Perhaps it was the colors/grading used or how it was edited together. Or maybe it was that the camera was too shaky and nauseating. Think on how you imagine doing it differently. How would you have rewritten the story to make it engaging, and who do you think would be a right cast for it? What exactly in the color scheme or editing would you have changed, and how much camera shake do you feel is creatively appropriate.

> *"Successful people ask better questions, and as a result, they get better answers."—Tony Robbins*

Judgement Rooted in The Now

Also watch films that other people down right tell you not to watch. The definition of what is good and bad keeps evolving with time and people.

---

[23] I suggest listening to Naval Ravikant's three and a half hour long podcast on 'How to Get Rich' at https://nav.al/rich. Transcript is also available. Getting rich might not be why one starts on the journey of filmmaking, but in making any art what we are essentially creating is wealth, something of value to another person.

It is easier to spot these things in someone else's film than in a film that we painstakingly created. According to your sensibilities think on what you believe could have been done differently. In doing so, you are not only developing your judgement, but also developing it rooted in the now, for your audience.

Over Time

Previously you might not have been able to point out why you do not like something or why you liked it. But in attempting to answer these questions, over time you start building your own vocabulary of what is good and bad and why it is so. You slowly start to realise what your personal taste is and this might later help you develop your own signature. Just as you are at the end ask the same questions about this book. What did you find useful, what were those that you felt were not true, what could you have improved?

Decisions taken on set are mainly taken on the foot. We rarely get the time to fully analyse how a decision you take would later turn out. Which is one advantage that experienced filmmakers have over beginners. Doing your own analysis, along with the films you make, is one way you can cover that gap and get better faster. It is in those high pressure situations on set that all the years of effort you put into cultivating your judgement as a filmmaker come to shine. You will know what you like and don't, what worked before and didn't. You will also know if your decision will work with your audience or not. To someone but you, it would look like you were born to do this.

How to Keep The Audience in Mind

Once you are done with your script, send it to 5 friends you trust. If you have access to filmmakers you trust, then send it to them too. Ask them for an honest feedback and listen, because they will tell you what they did not like. Had you gone and made that film you would have heard the exact same things from the audience. Now you get to hear it way in advance and for free. It is not an easy thing to listen to someone criticise something you created. But nonetheless we will hear it one day. Better to correct it before hand.

Your friends might not be able to tell you what to correct, that is your job. But they will tell you when they felt bored, when something didn't feel right. Ask them when they skipped pages. These will tell you portions that you need to work on. Repeat the same process of getting feedback not only with the updated scripts, but also with the different versions of your film's edit. It was by going through that that we were able to get *Munnariv* to its current form. As you become an experienced filmmaker, and you've seen your film with audiences, you will develop your own sense of what works in your craft and what doesn't.

* * *

Blanking Out On The Set of My First Short Film

Like many people starting out, my first short film was made with friends called Boomerang[24]. It was nothing like a set. Just 4 guys hanging out at a friend's place, shooting some things for a day on some camera. Nobody cared or payed any attention. We were doing our own thing.

---

[24] My first short film made with friends, called *Boomerang* youtu.be/ProaRWKAT2c

As we were all friends, the channels of communication were open. By the time I decided to do my second short film called *Thengil Keravo*[25] (meaning could you climb the coconut tree), I was out of college and all my friends were out working. The story needed elder characters. So I brought in my parents, few of my relatives, 2 or 3 of my free friends and their parents and relatives. It was to be a one day quick shoot in three locations close by. Besides them helping out, I was the whole crew.

Briefing My First Short Film Team

I remember the morning of the shoot. No one knew what the story was, their characters and dialogues. I had to brief them. Everyone had gathered around me in front of our first location. A crowd of maybe 10. How I wish someone was shooting behind the scenes that day, then I could have shown you my plight. I knew what I was supposed to do. But nothing was coming to my mind. I couldn't open my mouth. I was so scared. Even if I did say something I do not know if it would have made any sense. My mind was blank. Then I remembered that thankfully I had a bound script and I had printed it out. So I turned to read it. At least then I could say something.

The Future Director

I took it out and looked at the script I had typed and printed myself. I could see the letters, but I could not read even a single word. It looked like gibberish. The letters seemed liked blotches of black ink on white paper. My parents were right there in the crowd, on my first 'set', looking to see this future film director and what a screwup I was being. I personally knew everyone in front of me. I wasn't in a crowd of unknown

---

[25] My second short film called *Thengil Keravo* youtu.be/HOXBYI-5kug

technicians. These were my friends and relatives. Even then! Oh my god, what a day! I turned to my friend beside me, who was sort of being an Assistant Director that day. I asked him in his ear if he could narrate the story. Which he did. Somewhere halfway through his narration, my mind cleared. I came out of my own head, my fears and got into the story. I took over from him and then the day went ahead smooth. I was there present. It felt natural.

Learning From Experience

By my third short film I was prepared for my mind blanking out. Instead of having everything written, I had everything storyboarded, stick figure sketches. Once I saw the frame I saw the whole film and knew what part of the film that particular scene was. I also had the script printed in English, which I am more used to reading than Malayalam. I no longer feared the blotches of black ink on the white paper. By the time I was shooting *Munnariv*, my debut feature, I did not even need storyboards. I also had a crew of people helping me out. Though small, it wasn't just me doing everything, from calling 'camera rolling', 'action' and 'cut' as before. You might be able to learn a lot from these articles and tutorials, but it pales in comparison to what you learn by actually doing it. Do your thing your way and learn by making your mistakes.

* * *

Giving Back

By sharing we get to grow beyond ourselves. If you do follow these principles and get to make a film, I request you to shoot some behind the scenes footage. Not all aspiring filmmakers get to be on set. We might not always be able to accommodate them. But if you can shoot footage of your days on set, the different challenges you face everyday and how you solve them, and share these on YouTube or wherever, those can be invaluable to others.

Unfortunately we could not shoot much during *Munnariv*, but I will definitely do so in my following films. And once this book has served you its purpose, hand it over to someone else who needs it. Together let's improve the culture and knowledge on filmmaking.

* * *

My Top Secret Master Plan

1. Make a 5 lakh film and earn 10 lakhs with it
2. Use that money to make a 10 lakh, technically sound film
3. Use that money to make an even more brilliant 20 lakh film
4. Keep growing doing this, while entertaining the hearts, minds and souls of all of us, by making brilliant pieces of art

It is a long journey. I want you to go out and make your film as well so that we all can have each other's company. Taking one step at a time, let us all walk steadily towards our dreams and goals.

If you have read so far and found value in this book, may I request you to take a couple of minutes more to rate and review this book? If you have suggestions or thoughts you want to share, write to me at hi@iashik.com. Thanks in advance. Wishing you the very best!

Tools and Resources List

Preproduction

- Celtx v3, old downloadable desktop client - Scriptwriting, Script breakdown, Scheduling - Free
- Storyboarder – Easy to use storyboard application - Free

Production

- iPhone SE
- Moondog Labs 1.33X Anamorphic Lens – for iPhone 5/5S and iPhone SE
- Moondog Labs 52mm Filter Mount – for Clamp-on Anamorphic Lenses
- Hoya 52 mm Polariser Filter
- Tiffen 52 mm to 58 mm Step-Up Adapter
- Tiffen 58DVFMK3 58 mm DV Film Look Filter Kit 3
- Solar power bank by Poweradd
- Cheap phone holder for the tripod
- Sonia Pro 777 Tripod
- Zhiyun Smooth Q

Postproduction

- Blackmagic Design's DaVinci Resolve - Editing, Dubbing, Color Grading, Delivery - Free
- Neat Video - Plugin for removing noise from video - $60 to $110 (₹5,000 to ₹8,000), One time purchase
- False Color Plugin for DaVinci Resolve - Human eyes is more sensitive to changes in luminance level. Buy to set black levels, unless you have a professional calibrated monitor -
- Subtitle Edit - Easy to use software for creating subtitles - Free YouTube too can be used for free to create subtitles.
- HandBrake - Difficult to use, but powerful software for converting the film from one format to another - Free

Delivery

- Amazon Prime Direct
- Quiver - Get free estimates on VOD costs

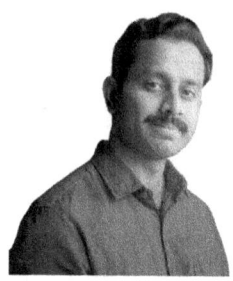

About the Author

Ashik Kumar Satheesh is a heart touching writer, film director and screenwriter, besides being an engineer. He founded and heads Ashik Arts LLP to fulfil his dream of making people's life meaningful, one story at a time.

Born in 1990, in Kerala, India, Ashik received attention for his early short film, *Dhaarna* (2017). After directing his first short film, *Boomerang* (2012), Ashik's next film came 3 years later, as he worked full time in Tata Consultancy Services, saving money to pursue his future ambitions.

In 2015, he resigned, traveled across the country, and came back to put his attention and focus entirely on filmmaking. Since then he has worked as Assistant Director to Award winning short films and feature films, like *Ottamuri Velicham* (2017). He made 8 short films of his own, to hone his craft.

Ashik started writing stories as a child. Unaware of his artistic talents, he went on to secure a First Class in Engineering. An avid reader and photographer he created his first short film with his friends from college, many of whom are now producing his debut feature.

Ashik's films are known for its brilliant stories, depth of characters, and his audacious filmmaking techniques. Both *Dhaarna* and *Munnariv* had narrative structures that captured people's attention from the get-go, with Munnariv receiving much of its attention for being a rare science fiction film in Malayalam.

The director's work focuses on protagonists who try come to their identities working through complex challenges.

A native of God's Own Country, Kerala, he lives with his parents in Kochi. He loves this place, its people and believes it to be a melting pot of religions and cultures, with innumerable stories that a global generation can look up to.

You can connect with me on:

🌐 https://iashik.com

🐦 https://twitter.com/AshikSatheesh

📘 https://www.facebook.com/ashiksatheesh

Subscribe to my newsletter:

✉ http://eepurl.com/ge59ov